A Pho
MU~~~~ ~~~~~OMS
OF BRITAIN AND EUROPE

Paul Sterry

First published in the UK in 1995 by
New Holland (Publishers) Ltd
24 Nutford Place, London W1H 6DQ

Copyright © 1995: New Holland (Publishers) Ltd

All rights reserved. No part of this publication may be reproduced, stored in a retrieval system, or transmitted, in any form or by any means, electronic, mechanical, photocopying, recording or otherwise, without the prior written permission of the copyright owners and publishers.

ISBN 1 85368 300 0 (hbk)
     1 85368 415 5 (pbk)

Editor: Charlotte Fox

Designed and typeset by D & N Publishing, Ramsbury, Wiltshire

Reproduction by Daylight Colour Arts (Pte) Ltd, Singapore
Printed and bound in Malaysia by Times Offset (M) Sdn Bhd

Front cover photograph: Fly Agaric (Paul Sterry)
Back cover photograph: Clouded Agaric (Paul Sterry)
Title page photograph: Conical Wax-cap (Paul Sterry)

Photographic Acknowledgements
All the photographs in this book were supplied by Nature Photographers Ltd. Most were taken by Paul Sterry, the exceptions being the following:
S. C. Bisserot 83l, 88l; Frank V. Blackburn 14l, 15l, 17u, 24l, 30l, 31l, 39l, 40u, 46l, 47u, 49l, 50l, 51l, 62u, 63u, 64u, 76u, 79l, 82u, 95u, 95l, 103l, 104u, 107u, 110u, 111u, 115l, 117l, 118l, 121l, 127u,128l, 130l, 137l; Derick Bonsall 37u, 52l, 96u, 129u; Brinsley Burbidge 48l, 57u, 66u, 73l, 81l, 83u, 104l, 126u, 132l, 139u; Robin Bush 16u, 19l, 20u, 21u, 23l, 26l, 27u, 29u, 32u, 32l, 35l, 43l, 44u, 56u, 62l, 70l, 72l, 74l, 80l, 87u, 90l, 91u, 93u, 94l, 101l, 103u, 111l, 114u, 119l, 122l, 135u; Kevin Carlson 77u; Andrew Cleave 39u, 49u, 51u, 59u, 80l, 81u, 97u, 101u, 105u, 108u, 113l, 120u, 124l, 128u, 129l, 138l; Ron Croucher 50u, 80l, 108l; C. H. Gomersall 71u, 85l, 98u, 113u; James Hyett 59l, 61u, 66l, 68l, 72u, 76l, 77l, 78u, 127l; E. A. Janes 16l, 18u, 25l, 33l, 38u, 42l, 117u, 122u, 133l; D. Osborn 30u, 37l, 44u, 46u, 56u, 57l, 58l, 60u, 68u, 75u, 75l, 84l, 87l, 90u, 94l, 119u, 125l; Jim Russell 125u; Don Smith 109l; Andrew Weston 23u, 64l, 71l, 80u.
u = upper, l = lower.

The author and publishers believe the information in this book to be correct and accurate at the time of going to press. Neither the author nor the publisher can accept any legal liability or responsibility for any errors or omissions that may result. It is essential to be absolutely sure of the identification of any species of mushroom before eating it. If there is any doubt at all of its edibility, do not eat the mushroom.

Contents

Introduction

There can be few people with an interest in the countryside who have not noticed mushrooms and toadstools on their rambles along country lanes or through autumn woodlands. For some, the interest may be a passing one - curiosity about an especially colourful species or concern about whether a particularly delicious looking specimen is really edible. For others, the study of fungi may be taken more seriously, with whole day excursions becoming fungal forays. Whatever your level of interest, however, the fungi of Britain and Europe provide enough scope for full-time pursuit and enough variety to capture the imagination of the more general naturalist. This book is intended to cater for as many levels of interest as possible and to help the enthusiastic amateur mycologist identify the most common and widespread or spectacular and distinctive species of the region.

There are several thousand species of fungi to be found throughout Europe, including the British Isles. Many are microscopic and, though they are important to the agriculturalist because of the damage they do to crops, they are beyond the scope of this book. Of the larger fungi, there are at least two thousand species, of which nearly a thousand are common somewhere. Selecting an appropriate range of species for a book of this size can, not surprisingly, pose a problem especially since many of those that are common in the north are rare in the south and vice versa. To make the book as useful as possible, the species list has been made on the basis not only of their abundance in parts of the region but also on the range over which they are found in Europe.

The species included in the book are mainly those that are recognised easily in the field without the need for a microscope. Most are large, some are positively enormous while at the other extreme, a few are small or even minute. What they have in common, however, are the shared characters that make them fungi; a group of organisms that are neither plants nor animals in the strict sense. They also display a wealth of extraordinary shapes and characters worthy of devoted study.

How to use this book

The main part of this book, between pages 14 and 139, is devoted to species identification and 252 species are covered. They are arranged in groups according to the accepted modern classification of fungi and follow the order of other recent field guides. Fungi that have tubes are followed by those with gills. Next come the stomach fungi, most of which look like round balls, then the bracket and related fungi, followed by the jelly fungi. Last are the disc fungi and so-called 'burnt' fungi. In addition to the species normally covered by fungus field guides, two representatives of

4

an unrelated group, the slime moulds, are also included; they are commonly encountered and invariably invite curiosity. Each species described has a colour photograph and descriptive text.

The photographs
Fungi are notoriously difficult to illustrate. Almost every aspect of their appearance can and does vary, not only between specimens of the same species but even within the life of a single individual. Some change colour as they mature or age and some even look different depending on the humidity of the air. Size can also vary tremendously, as can the shape of the cap or the stature of the stem. When selecting photographs, careful attention has been placed on trying to choose an image which best conveys the appearance of a particular species at all stages in its life. Where this is impossible to depict in a single picture, the text has been carefully written to complement the photographic information.

The descriptions
In order to make comparison between species as easy as possible, the text has been written in a standard order wherever possible. First comes the common English name which, of course, many species of fungi do not have. This is followed by the scientific name comprising two words. Take, for example, the familiar fly agaric, *Amanita muscaria*. The first word applies to the genus in which the fungus belongs eg. *Amanita*, the agaric genus. The second denotes the particular species to which the fungus belongs. For some species, a second genus name or even second genus and species names will appear in brackets. In these cases, the names have recently been altered and the name in brackets will help when referring to other text books on the subject.

The next piece of information is a measurement. For the gill- and pore-bearing fungi, and many other species, this is the height in centimetres and is usually the maximum height acheived unless otherwise stated. For some species, the width is a more appropriate measurement and is, therefore, supplied here.

Next comes the species description itself. Where appropriate, the dimensions, shape and colour of the cap are given throughout its life, followed by information on the gills, flesh and stem. Because of the extreme variability found in some species, as much information as possible is given to enable an identification to be made at any stage in the life of the fungus. The next information given refers to the distribution and habitat preferences of a particular species. The latter, both in terms of the habitat type and growing substrate, can be invaluable when trying to identify fungi. Lastly, the time of year at which the mushroom or toadstool is likely to be found is given, together with an indication of its edibility or otherwise.

What are fungi?

For centuries, the living world was classified into two main kingdoms - animal and plant - and, until comparatively recently, fungi were automatically included in the latter category. Although they bear a superficial resemblence to plants, fungi lack the pigment known as chlorophyll which is contained in green plants and which is used to manufacture food from sunlight energy, carbon dioxide and water. Instead, like animals, they obtain their energy through the break-down of organic matter, in most cases from decaying tissue but in some cases from living tissue. Furthermore, the hard parts of fungi are chemically closer to the chitin which forms the casing of insects than to lignin which forms the hard parts of plants. A third category for the living world - the fungal kingdom - had to be created, therefore, to house these extraordinary organisms.

A mushroom or toadstool is only the fruit body, or reproductive part, of the fungus, and a comparatively short-lived stage at that. The main part of the fungus comprises an extensive network of very fine threads, or hyphae, that branch, join and weave below the surface of the ground, forming the mycelium and breaking down decaying material for sustenance. In the same way, the bracket fungus that grows on a tree is the fruit body of a fungal mycelium which penetrates the substance of the wood.

Individual hyphae are too small to be seen with the naked eye, but often a number of hyphae will cluster together to form visible threads about the thickness of sewing cotton. Certain fungi form even thicker black threads like bootlaces, which are known as rhizomorphs; these may be seen under the loose bark of dead trees.

The mycelium is perennial and certainly persists in the soil for decades, probably for centuries or more. It plays an important part in the rotting down of the leaves that fall in the autumn and the return of the nutrients to the cycle of life; the same is true of decaying tree stumps and fallen timber.

Not all fungi limit themselves to the breakdown of decaying organic matter. Some, for example, send their hyphae down to the roots of trees and form a network within the outer layers of the finer roots. There, a mutual interchange of material, known as a mycorrhizal symbiosis, takes place to the benefit of both parties. It is believed that the fungal hyphae are able to take up and transfer to the tree, minerals such as phosphates. In return, they receive from the tree compounds which they themselves are unable to synthesise. Rather than regarding the fungal element in the soil as a threat, foresters now consider their presence to be of vital importance.

Identifying fungi

There is seemingly no limit to the variety of shapes, textures and colours of fungal fruit bodies. They range from cups to finger-like projections, from caps on stalks to irregular potato-like lumps buried in the ground, from soft jellies to brackets too hard to cut with a knife and from brilliant red to pure white. At first, this diverse array may seem bewildering to the would-be mycologist. However, by focussing attention on some of the key features, the chances of a successful identification are greatly improved.

Before you do anything, take careful note of the growing location of the fungus. If you are in a woodland, for example, decide what substrate it is growing on, ascertain the nature of the woodland you are in and identify the type of tree under which the specimen is growing. The diagram below shows the basic structure of a fungi.

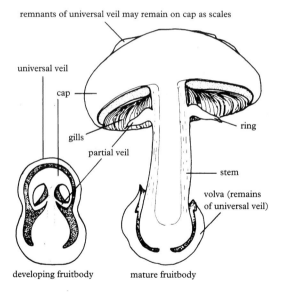

remnants of universal veil may remain on cap as scales

universal veil

cap

gills

partial veil

ring

stem

volva (remains of universal veil)

developing fruitbody   mature fruitbody

Next, study the fungus itself. In the case of a typical mushroom or toadstool fruit body, there will be a cap, supported and carried on a stem. Beneath the cap are the spore-bearing surfaces which may be either flat plates known as gills or tubes which end in openings known as pores. Note the arrangement of the gills: these may be decurrent, free or adnate. Note also the texture and

7

colour of both upper and under surfaces of the cap and also whether discolouration of milky exudate occurs on damage.

The stem should also be studied carefully. It may have a ring which can either be firm or fragile; this is formed from a membrane (the partial veil) which protects the developing gills of the young mushroom. The stem base may be contained in a bag, known as the volva. This is the remains of the sheath (the universal veil) that completely surrounds both the cap and stem as the fruit body grows, rupturing as the mushroom rises from the ground. Both veils may or may not be present and it is extremely important to recognise them if the fungus is to be identified correctly, particularly as the volva is a characteristic of some of the most poisonous species. A penknife or garden trowel can be used to lift the stem base out the ground.

Spore colour can also be an aid to identification but while the shade can usually be assessed from the colour of the gills, this is not more than a rough guide. A coating of spores on adjacent caps or on leaves close to the fungus may provide further evidence but an accurate assessment of colour can be made only by taking a sample. The stem should be cut off the specimen and the cap, moistened on the upper surface, laid gills down on a sheet of white paper and covered with a tumbler. After a few hours, a thick dusting of spores should have formed on the paper leaving a lasting impression of the gill pattern as well.

Corner tabs
These provide an at-a-glance reference to the species family groups enabling quick identification. See key below.

Pore fungi	Roll rims & relatives	Russulas	Milk-caps	Wax-caps	Oyster Mushroom & relatives
Funnel caps	Various gill fungi	Bonnet fungi	Ink caps	True mushrooms	Parasols
Agarics	Stinkhorns	Bird's nests	Puffballs	Chanterelle & relatives	Club fungi & relatives
Brackets	Jelly fungi	Morels	Disc fungi	Fire fungi	Slime moulds

Classification of fungi

Whilst all fungi have the same basic structure of hyphae and reproduce by means of spores, the way in which they distribute their spores separates them into two main divisions: these are the Basidiomycetes and the Ascomycetes.

Basidiomycetes allow their spores to fall into the passing air currents and so have to elevate their fruit bodies at least a short way above ground. The spores are formed on the stalks of cells known as basidia, and there are usually four to a cell. Ascomycetes form their spores in tubes known as asci which effect resemble gun barrels and usually point upwards. When ripe, the spores are forcibly ejected for several millimetres, which is enough to get them airborne. A third division of the fungal world, the slime moulds or Myxomycetes, has two representatives in this book for curiosity's sake, but their detailed classification and structure is outside the scope of this book.

Perhaps fortunately, very few spores germinate or at least develop into further organisms. For this reason, they are produced in enormous numbers, an average mushroom producing from 10 to 20 thousand million spores.

The Basidiomycetes

Within this group, five sub-divisions are considered in this book. These are the Boletales or fungi with pores, the Agaricales or gilled fungi, the Gasteromycetes or 'stomach fungi', the Aphyllophorales or bracket-type fungi and the Heterobasidiobmycetes or 'jelly fungi'. Wherever possible, common English names have been used.

The Boletales
With the exception of two rare species, all European members of this group grow on the ground and all form mycorrhizal associations with plants, mainly trees. They have the typical 'toadstool' shape and on the under surface of the cap they have tubes instead of gills which open as pores. Genera covered in this book include:

Boletus – with a dry cap and stem that may be covered with small dots or a fine net.

Suillus – with a cap that is slimy in wet weather and a smooth stem.

Leccinum – with a dry cap and scaly stem.

Strobilomyces – with a scaly cap and stem.

The Agaricales

These too have a typical 'toadstool' shape but have gills on the underside of the cap, not tubes; spores are formed on the surfaces of the gills. A few Agaricales have lateral stems but in most the cap is raised from the ground on a vertical stem. Some of the larger genera covered in this book include:

Lactarius – known as 'milk-caps' because when the caps or gills are broken, a milky juice exudes. The taste of the milk and whether or not it changes colour can be useful in identification. The gills are thick, adnate or decurrent, but never free.

Russula – many species form archetypal 'toadstools' with rounded, often brightly coloured caps and generally white stems. The flesh is brittle and the gills are white to yellow, in most species running all the way from the stem to the edge of the cap.

Hygrophorus and Hygrocybe – collectively known as the 'Wax-caps'. The gills are thick, well-spaced and waxy-looking. Many are brightly coloured and they vary in size from small to medium-sized fungi and in shape from a rounded cone to a flat-topped inverted cone. In moist weather the cap is slippery.

Amanita – contains some of the most poisonous and distinctive fungi. These fungi possess a volva which can be large and tough, fragile or reduced to a series of rings on the lower stem. Most species have a ring but this is sometimes hidden in certain species.

Lepiota – whitish fungi with a more-or-less scaly cap, white and free gills, and a ring. The genus is now divided into the large and edible species called Macrolepiota and the small and inedible species which retain the name Lepiota.

Collybia – a large genus, members of which are important decay organisims in woodland ecology. The white gills are either free of, or lightly attached to the stem, which is usually tough, giving rise to the group name of 'Tough-shanks'.

Clitocybe – characterised by having white gills which are markedly decurrent. The cap is often funnel-shaped and the stem short.

Mycena – small, white-gilled fungi, the gills mostly adnate. The caps are usually conical but may open flat later and the stems are long and slim. Some species exude a sap when cut.

Coprinus – characterised by having gills and caps which slowly liquify, the spores being washed away by the rain.

The Stomach Fungi

A very varied group which form their spores on a network of hyphae and basidia which is initially contained in the fruit body. These may be expelled through a central opening, as in the Puffballs, or released by disintegration of the casing. In the Stinkhorns, the spores are contained in a slime carried on a stem.

The Bracket Fungi and relatives

These are fungi without true gills although some members of the group may appear to have them. Perhaps the most illustrative is the genus Stereum, which consists of horizontally disposed plates with the spore-bearing surface on the underside.

The Jelly Fungi

An aptly-named group whose fruit bodies are usually elastic in nature. The spores are formed internally but are borne on basidia. The species described are all parasitic or saprophytic on wood.

The Ascomycetes

The larger Ascomycetes dealt with in this book can be divided into two groups, the Discomycetes or 'Disc Fungi', and the Pyrenomycetes or 'Burnt Fungi'.

The Disc Fungi

These are characteristically saucer-shaped and of various sizes from less than a millimetre to several centimetres in width. The spore-producing layer is borne on the upper surface. Some Disc Fungi, among which are the Morels, have a stem carrying a convoluted bead.

The Burnt Fungi

These generally have a black, crusty appearance which gives them the common English name. They bear their spores in asci which point inwards to a flask-shaped hollow and make their way to the air through an opening in the flask. In addition, some species produce conidiospores, which are in effect the budding off of the ends of the hyphae; they may form a white dust on the surface of the fruit body.

Studying fungi

The study of fungi can be a fascinating pastime and one that can take you to a wide range of places and terrains. Fungi have exploited almost every conceivable habitat and ecological niche. Good numbers and variety can be found on heathlands, in grassland, on lawns and beside paths.

The best opportunities for the fungus hunter occur, without doubt, in our woodlands. Although almost any type of wood can be good, mature and undisturbed areas are usually best. Leaf litter beds and decaying stumps are normally very productive while areas that have been cleared of fallen wood are, necessarily, poor in species. You should also bear in mind that different species are adapted to coniferous woods as compared to deciduous woods and very few occur in both.

Fungal hunting is also a pursuit that can be enjoyed more-or-less throughout the year, although the autumn months are the most productive. The months of August, September and October are perhaps the highlights in the fungus hunter's year and the best flushes of numbers and variety will come a few days after prolonged heavy rain. If the preceding spring and summer have been wet then so much the better; drought years offer poor yields of fungi.

Searching for fungi is not always as easy as it sounds. When seen in the field, and from above, many appear far less distinctive than they do in illustrations; in fact, some have stems that may be almost completely concealed by leaf litter or debris. Others are remarkably camouflaged on the woodland floor. One good way to increase your chances of finding these more cryptic species is to lie flat on the woodland floor yourself. At ground level, many more mushrooms and toadstools will be easily seen.

Because of the nature of fungi, they make poor collection specimens: they often shrivel, distort and discolour, and some even putrify. Fortunately, however, they do make excellent photographic subjects and a good collection can soon be built up in a season. You will need a macro lens on your camera in order to take close-up shots of some of the smaller species. A tripod which enables you to photograph at ground level is also invaluable since fungi often grow in gloomy settings where light levels are low and slow shutter speeds are needed. A small flash gun can be useful to brighten up the subject and it is sometimes an idea to deliberately over expose the photo by, say, a quarter of a stop if shooting in dark woodland.

Many fungus enthusiasts like to finish off a hard day's fungus forays by consuming the more edible specimens they encounter. While eating fungi can be a rewarding and mouth-watering way to end the day, the dangers of misidentification of poisonous species cannot be overemphasised. The simple rule with fungi is 'If in any doubt, do not eat'.

Fungus enthusiasts should also bear in mind the vulnerability of some species. In some parts of Europe, and indeed also in a few areas of Britain, fungi are collected with such enthusiasm and in such numbers that this may be having an effect on the populations of particularly edible or spectacular species. While there is no doubt that habitat destruction is a far more immediate and widespread threat, it would be a shame if enthusiasts exacerbated the problem. So never take more than you need and always try to identify specimens *in situ* if possible.

Glossary

Adnate Gills which are attached to the stem.

Agaricale Fungus with gills.

Ascus Microscopic part of an Ascomycete which fires the spores.

Basidium Spore-bearing part of a Basidiomycete

Cap Upper part of a mushroom.

Decurrent Gills that run down the stem.

Free Gills which do not touch the stem.

Fruit body Reproductive part of the fungus.

Gills Flat, spore-bearing plates beneath the cap.

Gluten Slimy coating on some fungus bodies.

Hyphae Fine threads composing the entire fungus.

Mycelium Network of threads (hyphae) which form the unseen part of the fungus.

Partial veil Membrane protecting the developing gills.

Pores Openings of the spore-bearing tubes in the Boletales.

Rhizimorphs Thick, black threads formed from hyphae.

Ring Formative remnant of hyphae surround the stem.

Spore Single-celled equivalent of a seed in flowering plants.

Tubes Spore-bearing structures in the Boletales found beneath the cap.

Universal veil Sheath which surrounds the cap and stem of the developing fungus.

Volva Remains of the universal veil, forming a bag at the base of the stem.

Cep or Penny Bun *Boletus edulis* Height up to 20cm

This distinctive toadstool is popular with cooks throughout Europe. The brown cap averages 12cm across, is rounded when young, becoming flatter with age. The surface is rather mealy at first but becomes smooth and acquires a greasy texture when wet. Pores are white, becoming creamy-grey and then yellow. Flesh is white and pleasant smelling. The stem is fat and bulbous; the surface is pale grey, covered with a white net, especially at the top. Widespread in Europe, including Britain. Found in woodland, usually under beech and oak and appears from August to November. It is edible and delicious.

Red-cracking Bolete *Boletus chrysenteron* Height up to 10cm

A common toadstool with a distinctive cap up to 10cm across. Cap is hazel-brown, initially with a slightly velvety texture, this soon wearing off to leave a smooth surface, cracking to reveal bright red flesh beneath. Pores are dirty yellow and the flesh, which is of medium thickness, is cream or straw, with a thin reddish layer immediately beneath the cuticle. The stem is usually flushed red throughout most of its length except for the very top which is yellowish. Occurs across Europe, appearing from August to November in deciduous woodland. Although edible, it is not recommended.

14

Bay Bolete *Boletus badius (Xerocomus badius)*
Height up to 15cm

An aptly named species with a cap, usually 10cm across, which occurs in various shades of tan, from buffish-orange to deep chestnut. At first, the cap is domed but becomes flatter with age; the surface is textured at first but becomes smooth. Pores are creamy-yellow but bruise greenish-blue. Flesh is whitish but, when cut, acquires a bluish tinge. The stem, which is usually of equal diameter along its length, is buffish-yellow but netted with dark brown veins. Widespread in Europe, occurring in both deciduous and coniferous woodlands from September to November. Considered delicious.

Boletus erythropus Height up to 15cm

A common and rather colourful toadstool. Cap, usually 10-15cm across, is tan or chestnut in colour with a slightly mealy texture at first, becoming sticky with age; it is domed but becomes flatter. Pores are reddish-orange but bruise bluish. The yellowish flesh stains blotchy blue when cut and exposed to the air. The stem is fat and particularly swollen towards the base; its ground colour is yellowish but the surface is suffused with red. Widespread in Europe, including Britain, growing in both coniferous and deciduous woodlands. It appears from August to November. Inedible.

15

Boletus impolitus (*Xerocomus impolitus*) Height up to 12cm

A robust toadstool which could be mistaken for the Bay Bolete when seen from above. Cap is up to 12cm across, is buffish-tan and usually mottled with a suffusion of darker, reddish-brown. Bright yellow pores stain and bruise darker. Flesh is white with a faint yellow tinge. Unlike the Bay Bolete, the stem is fat and bulbous; it is brownish and mottled with dark reddish-brown towards the base. Local in southern Britain but more widespread on the continent. Grows in deciduous woodlands, especially under oak, and appears from July to September. Although edible, it may be mistaken for other, inedible species.

Boletus luridus Height up to 15cm

The cap of this local species is up to 12cm across, buffish or light brown with a textured, then smooth surface. Orange-buff pores bruise bluish. Flesh is whitish with a faint yellow tinge but slowly stains bluish when cut and exposed to the air. The particularly variable stem can be fat and bulbous or comparatively elongated; it is yellowish-tan in colour with a fine network of red veins, most pronounced towards the base. Grows in deciduous woodlands, especially under beech. Appears from August to October and is fairly common in mainland Europe but less so in Britain. Inedible.

Boletus parasiticus (Xerocomus parasiticus) Height up to 10cm

An intriguing parasitic species found growing on the Common Earth-ball (*Scleroderma citrinum*). The cap, which is domed at first but becomes irregularly shaped with age, is 3cm across and tan to rich-brown in colour. Pores are yellowish, becoming orange-brown with age. Flesh is yellowish and does not discolour when cut and exposed to air. The stem is straw-coloured and either a uniform diameter along its length or tapering towards the base. Widespread and always local in Europe, its precise distribution is dependent upon the occurrence of its host fungus. Found in woodlands and heaths, and appears from August to October. It is not edible.

Red-capped Bolete *Boletus versicolor* Height up to 8cm

The cap of this colourful and attractive toadstool is up to 5cm across. It is usually bright red, sometimes with a slightly mealy texture. Pores are pale lemon-yellow turning bluish when bruised. Yellowish flesh does not stain when cut and exposed to the air. The stem, which is usually uniform in diameter along its length or slightly tapering towards the base, is yellowish but strongly tinged with red, especially towards the base. Widespread in Europe but rather local in Britain. It grows in deciduous woodland, especially under oak, and appears from September to November. Although edible, it is best avoided.

17

Boletus subtomentosus (Xerocomus subtomentosus)
Height up to 9cm

This rather nondescript Bolete shares characters with several other similar species. Cap, up to 10cm across, is buffish-tan with a mealy or almost velvety texture; the margin of the cap is sometimes paler. Pores are yellow and bruise darker. Flesh is pale, grading from whitish in the cap to creamy-buff in the stem. Stem is sometimes slightly tapering towards the base; it is buffish in colour with a suffusion of reddish-brown. Fairly common and widespread in Europe, including Britain, and grows in deciduous woodland from September to November. Edible but best avoided.

Boletus pruinatus Height up to 10cm

A rather local toadstool of mature woodlands. The cap, which is usually 5-8cm across, is domed at first, but becomes flatter with age. It is light brown to deep chestnut in colour, often appearing rather reddish around the margin. The pores are pale lemon-yellow and may bruise bluish. Flesh is also pale lemon-yellow and the stem is yellowish but flushed with red towards the base. Widespread but local in Europe growing mainly in beech woods but also under oak. It appears in October and November. It is edible but best left because of its comparative rarity.

18

Peppery Bolete *Boletus piperatus* Height up to 10cm

A distinctive species both in terms of appearance and its peppery taste. The cap, which is 5-10cm across, is domed at first but spreads flatter with age. It is dull orange-brown in colour with a shiny appearance when dry and a sticky texture when wet. Pores are orange-tan. Flesh is pale but stains deeper yellow towards the base and the stem is dull orange-brown, concolorous with the cap, and comparatively slender and of uniform diameter. Widespread but local in Europe, usually in birch woodlands or scrubby heaths. Appears from September to November. It is edible, but should be cooked.

Slippery Jack *Suillus luteus* Height up to 12cm

The chestnut-coloured cap, 8cm across, is covered in gluten which, as its common English name suggests, becomes very slippery in wet weather. The pores and tubes are dirty yellowish and small. Flesh is pale and almost white, greyish at the base. Stem is whitish at the base and yellower near the top; the colours are separated by a ring which is initially pale but darkens almost to the cap colour. Common and widespread in Europe although always associated with conifers. It appears from September to November and is edible if the gluten is removed.

Suillus bovinus Height up to 10cm

The cap of this robust species is rounded or bulbous at first expanding to a dome-shape with age. Cap is pale cinnamon with a paler margin and the surface is covered with slippery gluten. Pores are pale grey to cinnamon; they are large and irregular, with smaller ones inside, and slightly decurrent. The flesh is slightly yellowish becoming clay-pink on exposure to air; it is darker towards the base of the stem. The stem is parallel and cinnamon. Widespread in European pine woods, mostly under Scots Pine. It appears from September to November and is edible but best avoided.

Suillus variegatus Height up to 12cm

A fairly large and common species. The cap is very rounded at first but becomes expanded and flattened with age. It is light tan in colour and the surface is slightly scaly although sticky when wet. The pores are brown, a darker shade than the cap. The flesh is pale, almost whitish, but becoming darker towards the base of the stem and the stem is yellowish-brown and stout. Fairly widespread in Europe, including Britain, but is confined to conifer woodland and appears from September to November. Although edible, it is not a very popular taste.

Larch Bolete *Suillus grevillei* Height up to 10cm

The cap, which expands to a diameter of up to 10cm, is rounded-conical becoming more flattened with age. It is orange-tan in most specimens but older examples may be paler. Pores are yellow but bruise orange-brown. The flesh is pale yellow but more intense towards the base of the stem and the stem itself is yellowish with a whitish ring below which there are darker scales. As its common English name suggests, the Larch Bolete is invariably associated with larch woodland; it is, however, widespread in Europe and common where it occurs, being seen from August to November. Edible.

Brown Birch Bolete *Leccinum scabrum* Height up to 20cm

The cap of this fairly distinctive species feels as if it is filled with cotton wool. It is 7-15cm across, snuff-brown and rounded, more so in younger specimens. The pores are off-white and bruise darker. The flesh is white and does not discolour when cut and exposed to air. The stem is tall, white and covered with blackish scales. The Brown Birch Bolete is common and widespread in central and northern Europe including Britain, growing mainly in association with birch trees. It appears from late July to November and, although edible, is not worth considering.

Orange Birch Bolete *Leccinum versipelle* Height up to 25cm

The cap of this attractive toadstool, which averages 12cm across, is a rich orange-brown. It is dry to touch and much firmer than that of the Brown Birch Bolete. The cuticle of the cap often forms an overhanging skirt. Pores are small and greyish and the flesh is white, rapidly darkening to blue-green on being cut and exposed to the air; it becomes nearly black in both the stem and cap. The stem is white but covered with brownish-black scales and bruising black. Widespread and invariably found under birches. It appears from July to November and is edible.

Leccinum variicolor Height up to 10cm

This species often appears comparatively tall and slender. The cap, which is 5-9cm across, is grey-brown in colour and often mottled with darker markings; it is textured but slightly sticky when wet. The pores are whitish and small and the flesh is whitish but tinged with pinkish-yellow in the cap. The stem is usually long and slender; it is white but bears a network of dark scales. Widespread but local in Europe, usually growing in association with birch trees. It appears from August to October and is edible, but not particularly recommended.

22

Leccinum holopus Height up to 10cm

An unusual Bolete which often appears very pale. The cap, which is usually about 6cm across, is buff or very pale tan; older specimens become stained darker. The pores are whitish or very pale buff and bruise darker. The flesh is whitish and usually does not discolour when cut and exposed to air. The stem is whitish but often with varying amounts of dirty brown scales. *Leccinum holopus* is widespread in Europe but never common. It grows in Sphagnum moss under birch trees and appears in September and October. Although edible, it is not worth considering.

Old Man of the Woods *Strobilomyces floccopus*
Height up to 10cm

The cap of this unusual species is about 5-10cm, grey-brown in colour and covered in rough scales and white patches. The texture and colour recall that of dried mud. Pores are greyish-white and the flesh is whitish but stains reddish when cut and exposed to air. The stem is long and relatively slender, brown in colour and covered with large, rough scales. Rare and local in Britain but more widespread on the continent. It grows in both deciduous and coniferous woodland and appears from August to October. Although edible, it should not be picked because of its rarity.

23

Brown Roll-rim *Paxillus involutus* Height up to 10cm

A medium-sized species which, although bearing gills, is related to the Boletes. The cap averages 9cm in diameter and is downy brown; it maintains an inrolled margin for a long time then becomes funnel-shaped and reveals the decurrent, ochre gills. These can easily be pushed off the stem with a fingernail. The flesh and stem are similar in colour to the cap. Widespread in central and western Europe including Britain. It is found in woodland of many kinds but is usually associated with birch. It appears from September to November and is not edible.

False Chanterelle *Hygrophoropsis aurantiaca*
Height up to 7cm

A small and colourful toadstool which is similar in shape to many *Clitocybe* species but now in a different genus. The cap averages 5cm in diameter and is dark orange; it is usually an irregular funnel shape. The gills are orange, crowded and very decurrent. The flesh and stem are the same colour as the cap and gills. Common in Europe and grows under conifers, especially pines, appearing from September to November. It superficially resembles the highly edible Chanterelle but is unrelated. Although edible, this species has little flesh and no flavour.

Chroogomphus rutilus Height up to 15cm

An attractive fungus which is often much smaller than the maximum size. Cap is domed and rounded at first but soon expands and flattens, becoming almost funnel-shaped with a distinct umbo and a slightly inrolled margin; the cap is rich brown in colour. The gills are not crowded and are brownish and decurrent. The stem is yellowish-brown and contrastingly paler than the cap; the colour is most intense towards the base. Common and widespread in much of central and western Europe, growing in coniferous woodland. It appears from September to November and, although edible, is not worth considering.

Russula luteolacta Height up to 9cm

An attractive and rather local fungus. The cap is broadly domed at first but becomes flattened or even funnel-shaped with age, sometimes with a depressed centre; the cap colour is deep pinkish-purple although this may fade in some specimens. The gills are creamy-white. The flesh is white and the stem is white, sometimes with a pinkish flush towards the base; delayed yellow bruising occurs. Widespread but never particularly common. It grows mainly on heavy soils under deciduous trees such as hornbeam and sweet chestnut. It is poisonous.

Blackish-purple Russula *Russula atropurpurea*
Height up to 9cm

A common but unobtrusive species which is often overlooked on the woodland floor. The cap, which averages 7cm in diameter, is dark, almost black in the centre and reddish or purple around the sides. The gills are pale cream and are adnate and closely spaced. The flesh and the stem are white; there is a smell of apples and the taste is usually hot. Widespread in Europe, growing in deciduous woodland mainly under oak or beech where, in good seasons, it can be abundant. It appears from September to November and is edible if cooked.

Russula sardonia Height up to 8cm

A medium-sized, richly coloured species. The cap, which averages 7cm in diameter, is domed at first but becomes flattened with age; it is reddish to purple but sometimes brownish. The gills are primrose to golden-yellow and turn rose-pink with a drop of household ammonia; they are adnate. The flesh is thick and white and the stem is stout, white and usually overlaid with a strong purplish flush. The taste is hot and specimens often smell of stewed apples. Common and widespread, growing almost exclusively under pine trees. It appears from August to October and is not edible.

26

Russula caerulea Height up to 9cm

A clean-looking and attractive species. The cap, which averages 5cm in diameter, is rounded or conical in its early stages but becomes flattened with age, with a distinct and prominent umbo; It is deep reddish-purple in colour. The gills are creamy white and fairly widely spaced. The flesh and stem are white, the latter usually swollen towards the base and lacking any flush of colour. Locally common in Europe, being found growing under pine trees. It appears from August to October and is edible although perhaps not worth considering.

The Sickener *Russula emetica* Height up to 10cm

A brightly coloured and attractive species, often much smaller than its maximum size. The cap is domed in its early stages but expands and flattens, the centre sometimes becoming depressed; it is bright red and, when wet, is shiny and sticky. The gills are creamy white and the flesh is white but with a pink flush just below the cap cuticle. The stem is pure white and is usually slightly swollen towards the base. Widespread in Europe, including Britain, and grows under conifers. It appears from September to November. As its common English name suggests, it is poisonous.

27

Beechwood Sickener *Russula mairei* Height up to 7cm

A colourful species which is superficially similar to the Sickener although found in different habitats. The cap, which averages 4cm in diameter, is rounded at first but becomes flattened with age, and sometimes develops a depressed centre; it is bright red. The gills are white and adnate and the flesh is white. The stem is white and medium to tall, tapering only slightly upwards. Widespread in Europe, including Britain. It appears in September and October. As its common English name suggests, it grows almost exclusively under beech and is poisonous.

Common Yellow Russula *Russula ochroleuca*
Height up to 9cm

One of the most common fungi of lowland, broad-leaved woodlands. The cap, which averages 7cm in diameter, is ochre-yellow; it is domed at first but soon expands and flattens. Gills are pale cream and adnate, and the flesh is white and of medium thickness. Stem is white, greying with age. Occurs with a wide variety of trees, both deciduous and coniferous, although it is most abundant under the former. The exact shade of yellow makes it recognisable in the field once it has been encountered a few times. It appears from September to November and is not edible.

An attractive but rather local species. The cap, which averages 6cm in diameter, is lilac or greyish-purple; it is domed in its early stages and later becomes flattened, the centre sometimes depressed. The gills are white and rather close together, and the flesh is also white and watery. The stem is white and textured, the base occasionally being swollen. This species is most commonly associated with spruce trees, both when growing in mature plantations and as native forests on mainland Europe. It appears from September to November and, although edible, is not worth considering.

Charcoal Burner *Russula cyanoxantha* Height up to 9cm

A medium-sized species which often looks rather grubby. The cap, 7cm in diameter, is typically dull lilac with almost black patches. Gills are white, adnate, crowded and sometimes forked; they are distinguished by their greasy, flexible feel when the finger is rubbed over them. Flesh is white and of medium thickness. The stem, which is of average thickness, is white and hard and occasionally has a flush of the cap colour on it. Common and widespread in Europe including Britain, growing in deciduous woodland. It appears from July to November and is edible, although not very popular.

Milk-white Russula *Russula delica* Height up to 10cm

A distinctly pale and attractive Russula. The cap, which averages 10cm in diameter, is domed in its early stages but later expands and flattens; it is whitish in colour but sometimes irregularly blotched with darker patches. The gills are white and the flesh is white with a bitter, hot taste. The stem is white and robust. The Milk-white Russula is common and widespread in northern and western Europe including Britain. It grows in both coniferous and deciduous woodlands and appears from August to October. Edible when cooked.

Blackening Russula *Russula nigricans* Height up to 11cm

A large and thickset species which is extremely brittle. The cap, which averages 10cm in diameter, is whitish at first but soon darkens. Gills are white, widely-spaced and adnate with intermediate gills present. Stem is whitish and the flesh is hard and white but when cut it turns first greyish-pink and then dark grey; it has a hot taste. Eventually the whole fungus turns black but, because it is so slow to decompose, entirely black specimens are most commonly found. Grows in wooded habitats of all types and appears from July to November. Although edible, it is best avoided.

Grey Milk-cap *Lactarius vietus* Height up to 10cm

This variable fungus has a cap averaging 7cm in diameter. It is domed and flattened in its early stages but soon expands, becoming almost funnel-shaped; it is lilac-grey in colour and is slightly sticky when wet. Gills are greyish-buff and slightly decurrent and the stem is similar in colour to the cap but usually slightly paler. The flesh is pale buff and produces hot-tasting milk which is white at first but turns grey after a while. Common and widespread in Europe, found growing in deciduous woodlands especially under birch. Appears from September to November and is not edible.

Ugly Milk-cap *Lactarius turpis* Height up to 12cm

A grubby-looking fungus, as its name suggests. The cap, which averages 15cm in diameter, is dark olive-brown to dark grey; it is thick with a central depression when old. The gills are creamy and decurrent and the flesh is white but browning soon after being cut. Milk is white and hot tasting. The stem is paler than the cap; it is short and stout so that the cap lies almost on the ground. Common and widespread in Europe, including Britain. It grows mainly with birch and appears from September to November. It is not edible.

31

Woolly Milk-cap *Lactarius torminosus* Height up to 8cm

A medium-sized fungus with a distinctive texture. The cap, which averages 7cm in diameter, is orange, zoned with darker rings and covered with an orange-red coat like matted wool. Gills are white and slightly decurrent and the flesh is fairly thick. The milk is white and hot to taste. The stem is short to medium height and sturdy; it is pale flesh-coloured and lacks hairs. Widespread and fairly common in Europe, growing mainly in association with birch. It is poisonous and, although not deadly, should not be handled.

Saffron Milk-cap *Lactarius deliciosus* Height up to 8cm

This attractive species has a cap which averages 7cm in diameter and is zoned with orange and touches of green. The gills are pale pink and go green with age or when damaged; they are decurrent. Flesh is pale yellowish when first cut and the milk is carrot-coloured; it tastes mild or very slightly bitter. The stem is short, stout and greyish-buff, usually with depressed spots coloured orange. Found throughout Britain, and central and western Europe. It grows in woodlands, usually with pines, and appears from September to November. It is edible.

Slimy Milk-cap *Lactarius blennius* Height up to 8cm

A distinctive but unappealing species. The cap, which averages 6cm across, is various shades of brown and greenish-grey, often with blotches of darker colour in concentric zones. Rounded cap becomes funnel-shaped with age; the surface is slimy. Gills are white, becoming grey; they are slightly decurrent. The flesh is whitish and the milk is white at first, turning grey on the gill; it is intensely hot and acrid. The stem is short and sturdy, and greyish-cream in colour. Common and widespread, growing especially with oak or beech. It appears in September and October and is not edible.

Peppery Milk-cap *Lactarius piperatus* Height up to 10cm

The milk of this fungus has a distinctive, peppery taste. The cap, which averages 10cm in diameter, is domed and flattened in its early stages but expands and develops a depressed centre and inrolled margin; it is creamy-white in colour, the surface sometimes with small scales. Gills are yellowish and slightly decurrent and the stem is white and tapering towards the base. The flesh is white and the milk is white with a hot taste. Common and widespread in Europe, including Britain. It grows in deciduous woodland and appears from August to November. Although edible, it is not recommended.

33

Lactarius hepaticus Height up to 7cm

An easily overlooked fungus, the cap of which averages 5cm across. It is usually convex but can also be flattened and button-like; the colour is dull pinkish-orange or orange-buff and the texture is dry and smooth. Gills are slightly decurrent and buffish-orange. The flesh is buffish or off-white, darkening towards the base of the stem; the milk is white. The stem is the same colour as the cap and is tall and relatively slender. Widespread in central and western Europe including southern Britain. It grows under pines and appears from September to November. Inedible.

Lactarius tabidus Height up to 6cm

A small and rather attractive species. The cap, which averages 3.5cm in diameter, is orange-buff and flattened to convex, usually with a central pimple. The gills, which are yellower than the cap, are decurrent. The flesh is whitish and rather thin and the milk is white, turning yellow on a handkerchief but not on the gills themselves; the taste is slightly hot. The stem is relatively tall and similar in colour to the cap. Fairly widespread in Europe including Britain. It is found growing under deciduous trees, especially birch, and appears from September to November. It is not edible.

Rufous Milk-cap *Lactarius rufus* Height up to 8cm

The cap of this common fungus averages 6cm in diameter and is flattened in its early stages with the margin slightly inrolled. It soon expands, the centre becoming depressed with a noticeable umbo. Colour is brick-red to tan. Gills are buffish, paler than the cap, and slightly decurrent. The flesh is white and the milk is white, mild at first but leaving a burning after-taste. Stem is orange-buff becoming paler towards the base. Found mainly in coniferous woodlands but also occasionally in association with birch. Widespread in Europe, appearing from September to November. Inedible.

Scarlet Wax-cap *Hygrocybe coccinea* Height up to 6cm

A striking, red-coloured fungus. The cap, 3cm in diameter, is conical or rounded, expanding to an irregular, almost bell-like appearance with age. It may be slightly sticky in the early stages. Gills are bright red but with a paler, yellow margin; they are widely spaced. The stem is the same colour as the cap along most of its length but becoming paler towards the base. The flesh is reddish. Widespread in northern and western Europe including Britain. It grows in grassy places such as woodland rides and meadows, and appears from September to November. Inedible.

Conical Wax-cap *Hygrocybe conica* Height up to 7cm

The cap of this waxy toadstool averages 3cm in diameter, is distinctly conical and seldom opens fully. It starts by being yellow, orange or even red, but very soon begins to turn black unevenly. Gills, well hidden by the cap at first, are whitish and sinuate. The stem is tall and red while the flesh is yellowish-white. Eventually the whole fungus becomes completely black without, at first, losing its shape. Widespread species which grows in a range of grassy places. It appears from July to October and, although edible, is not worth considering.

Blackening Wax-cap *Hygrocybe nigrescens* Height up to 6cm

An attractive little species in its early stages but soon discolouring. The cap, which averages 4cm in diameter, is distinctly conical in its early stages but expands with age, the irregularly lobed margins sometimes splitting. It is deep orange-scarlet but this eventually turns black with age. The gills are widely spaced and yellow at first and the stem is yellowish at first. The flesh is yellow but bruises black. Widespread in Europe including Britain and grows in grassy places. It appears from August to October and, although edible, is not worth considering.

Crimson Wax-cap *Hygrocybe punicea* Height up to 7cm

An attractive, colourful toadstool. The cap, which averages 5cm across, is rounded-conical in shape and bright blood-red at first; the colour soon washes out with rain or frost, leaving the surface with the appearance of being covered with a white bloom. The gills are pale yellow, reddish at the base and adnate. The stem is yellowish-red becoming whitish towards the base; if split with a knife, the flesh is white. Widespread in Europe but seldom common; it is rare in Britain. It grows in grassland and appears from August to October. Although edible, it is not worth considering.

Hygrocybe langei Height up to 7cm

A rather scarce but attractive species. The cap, which averages 5cm in diameter, is rounded-conical at first but expands with age becoming flattened with a distinct umbo; it is yellow-orange in colour and rather waxy to touch. The gills are yellowish and paler than the cap. The stem is the same colour as the cap along most of its length but usually paler towards the base. The flesh is yellow. Widespread in north-western Europe including Britain but is always rather scarce. It grows in grassy places and appears from July to September.

Parrot Wax-cap *Hygrocybe psittacina* Height up to 5cm

A small and fairly common fungus. The cap, which averages 3cm in diameter, is creamy-yellow in colour but typically covered with a green, slippery gluten which persists patchily all over. The gills are adnate and white although they often look greenish because of the gluten collected between them. The flesh is whitish and the stem is yellowish but covered in the same green slime as the cap. Widespread in Europe, occurring in grassy places such as lawns and meadows; it appears from September to November. Although edible, it is not considered pleasant to eat.

Herald of Winter *Hygrophorus hypothejus* Height up to 8cm

Its late appearance gives rise to its English name. The cap, which averages 3.5cm in diameter, is dark greyish-brown but is covered with an olivaceous gluten, making it appear yellowish-orange; it is dome-shaped at first with an inrolled margin but expands and flattens with age. The gills are bright orange and widely spaced. The stem is relatively tall and yellowish-white in colour; it is coated with slippery orange gluten below the ring-zone. Widespread and common in Europe including Britain, growing in coniferous woodland. Appears in October or November and although edible, it is not worth considering.

Oyster Mushroom *Pleurotus ostreatus* Width up to 12cm

This bracket-shaped fungus has a rubbery texture and a passing resemblance to an oyster. Cap is up to 1cm thick and is extremely variable in colour, ranging from very dark grey at first but becoming lighter, or pale buff from the outset. The gills are whitish and widely spaced. Flesh is white with the gills reaching down the very short lateral stem almost to the base, which is hairy. The spores are pale lilac. Widespread and locally common, growing on deciduous trees and logs, especially beech. It appears from July to November and is edible and considered delicious.

Pleurotus cornucopiae Width up to 10cm

A bracket-shaped fungus found growing in dense clusters. Cap is up to 2cm thick and broadly rounded but with an irregular outline, the margin often torn or split; the cap colour is pale buffish-tan. Gills are the same colour as the cap and are widely spaced and often run down at least part of the stem which is usually curved and up to 4cm long. Flesh is white and has a faint smell of ammonia. Widespread but seldom particularly common. It is a woodland fungus which grows on tree-stumps and appears from June to September. This species is edible.

Panus torulosus Width up to 7cm

The cap of this robust fungus can be up to 2cm thick. It is usually irregularly rounded, the margin slightly inrolled and the centre rather depressed; the cap is orange-buff, older specimens having a cracked and flaky surface. The gills are decurrent and buffish-pink in colour. The stem, which can be up to 2cm long, is thickset and tapers towards the base; it is the same colour as the cap. Widespread in Europe including Britain, occurring in deciduous woodland where it grows on the stumps and dead and dying branches of trees. It appears from June to September. Inedible.

Tawny Funnel Cap *Clitocybe flaccida* Height up to 10cm

This aptly named species is tawny-coloured and funnel-shaped. The cap, which averages 8cm in diameter, is slightly rounded when young but soon expands and becomes funnel-shaped; there is a distinct umbo and the margins are inrolled and occasionally split. Cap colour is orange-brown, the texture is leathery. The gills are paler than the cap and decurrent. The stem is buffish-brown and swollen at the base, and the flesh is a similar colour. Widespread and common in Europe. In Britain grows in woodlands of all types, appearing from August to November. This species is edible but not recommended.

Clouded Agaric *Clitocybe nebularis* Height up to 12cm

A common, troop-forming woodland fungus. The cap, which is variable but averages 10cm in diameter, is grey and thick; it is rounded at first but soon expands and flattens. The gills are creamy and decurrent and the flesh is whitish. The stem varies in length but is sturdy and widens towards the base. The whole fungus has a strong, sweet smell. Widespread and often common, growing mainly in deciduous woodland. It appears in October and November. Although the young caps are edible, they can cause gastric disorders in some people and the species is best avoided.

Clitocybe geotropa Height up to 20cm

The appearance of this toadstool changes dramatically as it grows. The cap, averaging 17cm across in mature specimens, starts off as domed and button-shaped, with a prominent umbo; as it grows, it expands, flattens and becomes funnel-shaped, still retaining the umbo. Cap is buffish-yellow. The gills are decurrent and paler than the cap and the stem is tough and relatively slender; it is brownish-buff with a swollen, hairy base. The white flesh smells of hay. Common and widespread in north-western Europe. It grows in grassy woodland rides and appears from September to November. This species is edible.

Aniseed Toadstool *Clitocybe odora* Height up to 7cm

This attractive toadstool has a distinctive smell. The cap, 6cm in diameter, is rounded in its early stages but expands and flattens with age, sometimes becoming almost funnel-shaped, and develops a slight umbo; the cap colour is pale greenish-grey. Gills are pale greenish-white and decurrent. The stem is greenish-white with the base slightly swollen and woolly, and the flesh is whitish and has a strong taste of aniseed. Widespread and common in north-western Europe and beyond. It favours deciduous woodlands, often appearing beside trampled paths. It appears from August to November and is edible and good.

Clitocybe fragrans Height up to 7cm

A slender and rather delicate woodland toadstool. The cap, which averages 3cm in diameter, is button-shaped in its early stages but expands and flattens with age, becoming slightly depressed in the centre; it is pale buffish-brown with a darker centre and is hygrophanous. Gills are pale and adnate. The stem is slender and a similar colour to the cap; it is usually irregular rather than straight. The flesh smells of aniseed. Widespread in north-western Europe but seldom numerous. It grows in deciduous woodland and appears from September to November. Although edible, it is best avoided.

Honey Fungus *Armillaria mellea* Height up to 15cm

A common parasitic fungus, unpopular with foresters for the damage it causes. The cap averages 9cm in diameter and is rounded to flatly conical in shape; it is often honey-coloured, the surface is slightly scaly. Gills are whitish-yellow and decurrent. The stem, which is a similar colour to the cap, bears a ring and the flesh is white. Widespread in Europe. Grows in tufts on stumps and living trees, often destroying the latter; the lower caps in the clump are often coloured by white spores shed by the higher ones. It is seen mainly from September to November. Inedible.

Armillaria polymyces Height up to 15cm

Similar in appearance to, and easily mistaken for, the Honey Fungus. The cap, which averages 8cm in diameter, is rounded-conical to flattened in profile. Cap colour is pale reddish-brown with dark brown scales creating a dark centre. Gills are whitish-yellow and decurrent. The stem, which is similar in colour to the cap, bears a ring and often bears darker streaks. Widespread but seldom common and easily overlooked; it is one of several species that are closely related to the Honey Fungus. It grows on stumps and living trees and appears from September to November. Inedible.

Field Blewit *Lepista saeva* Height up to 8cm

The cap, which averages 8cm in diameter, is pale tan coloured; at first it is domed in outline but it soon expands and flattens, often rather irregularly when growing in clumps. The gills are the same colour as the cap and are adnate. The stem is lilac and usually rather swollen. The flesh, and indeed the whole fungus, is perfumed, the strong and pleasant smell perhaps being the best distinguishing feature of the species. Common and widespread in Europe including Britain. It grows in grassy places and appears in October and November. It is edible and widely considered to be delicious.

Wood Blewit *Lepista nuda* Height up to 10cm

An attractive fungus, usually flushed all over with bluish-lilac colour when young. The cap, which averages 8cm in diameter, is rounded-conical and lilac when young but soon expands, the cap colour fading to almost buff. Gills are a rich lilac colour when young but also fade with age. The stem is streaked with lilac and tends to broaden towards the base. Common and widespread in Europe occurring almost anywhere but is most often associated with deciduous trees. It appears relatively late, often in November and December. Edible although it can cause stomach upsets in some people.

The Deceiver *Laccaria laccata* Height up to 8cm

So-called because of the highly variable appearance of this fungus and the consequent problems this causes with misidentification. The cap, which averages 3.5cm in diameter, is tan-coloured but extremely variable both in terms of colour and shape. Gills are characteristically flesh-coloured, well-spaced and adnate. The stem is tall in relation to the size of the cap; it is fibrous, twisted and the same colour as the cap. Widespread in Europe, growing in almost any situation from deciduous and coniferous woods to cultivated lawns. It appears from July to November and, although edible, is best avoided.

Amethyst Deceiver *Laccaria amethystea* Height up to 10cm

As its common English name suggests, a variable species. The cap, which averages 3.5cm in diameter, is domed at first but soon expands and flattens, often rather irregularly; the cap colour is deep purple when wet but paler when dry. Gills are purple but become dusted with white spores when mature. The stem, which is usually rather irregular in shape, is the same colour as the cap with white hairs at the base. Common and widespread in Europe. It grows mainly in deciduous woodland and appears from September to November. Although edible, it is not recommended.

45

Plums and Custard *Tricholomopsis rutilans*
Height up to 10cm

Its unusual colouring gives this toadstool its imaginative name. The cap, which averages 7cm in diameter, has a ground colour of yellow but this is almost completely obscured by a layer of red-brown scales. The gills, which are adnate, are bright egg-yellow and the flesh is cream. The stem is slightly paler than the cap and has a more-or-less uniform thickness along its length. Widespread in Europe and locally common. It grows with conifers, especially pines, and is seen from July to November. It has bitter-tasting flesh and is not edible.

Tricholoma portentosum Height up to 10cm

A robust but easily overlooked fungus. The cap, which averages 7cm in diameter, is rounded at first but expands and flattens to become broadly conical; the cap colour is grey-brown, often with darker patches. The gills are off-white and the flesh is white and smells mealy. The stem is whitish and often rather irregularly formed. This species is widespread in Europe including Britain but it is seldom numerous. It is a woodland species, growing under conifers and appearing from August to October. Edible and considered delicious by some people.

Soap Tricholoma *Tricholoma saponaceum* Height up to 12cm

The whitish flesh of this irregularly formed fungus smells of soap. The cap, which averages 7cm in diameter, is rounded in its early stages but then expands and flattens, usually into a rather distorted shape. The cap colour is dark, ranging from grey-brown to almost black. Gills are pale yellow, wavy and widely spaced, and the stem is whitish, sometimes tinged pink near the cap and usually rather stout. Widespread in Europe including Britain. A woodland species, occurring both under coniferous and deciduous trees and appearing from August to November. Although edible, its smell and bitter taste render it unpalatable.

Tricholoma fulvum Height up to 8cm

Unpleasant smelling fungus which is easily recognisable due to its yellow gills. The slimy cap, which averages 7cm in diameter, is tawny, usually with slightly darker streaks radiating round the edge. The gills are adnate and yellow, developing brown spotting with age. The flesh is yellow and the stem is tallish and similarly coloured to the cap but paler at the top. This species is widespread in Europe including Britain. It is a woodland species and is usually associated with birch. It appears from September to November. Considered inedible due to its unpleasant taste and is best avoided.

47

A medium-sized, rather sombre-looking toadstool. The cap, which averages 7cm in diameter, is dark brown but becomes paler with age, usually showing a central umbo. The gills are white and sinuate and the flesh is white. The stem is fairly tall and white but with greyish fibrils, becoming darker with age and so retaining the contrast with the cap throughout the life of the fungus. *Melanoleuca melaleuca* is widespread in Europe and often common, growing in woodland settings, especially along grassy rides. It appears from August to November and, although edible, is best avoided.

Lyophyllum decastes Height up to 10cm

The cap of this distinctive fungus averages 7cm in diameter. It is varying shades of dirty brown with darker radial streaks. In its early stages, the cap is rounded-conical in outline but it expands and flattens with age. The gills are off-white; the flesh white. The tough and fibrous stem is whitish but darker towards the base. This species is often found growing in clumps and is common and widespread in northern Europe including Britain. It is found in woodland clearings and rides and appears from September to November. Although edible, it is probably best avoided.

St George's Mushroom *Calocybe gambosum*
Height up to 15cm

A distinctive spring species whose name comes from its appearance around St George's Day, 23rd April, and which has a superficial similarity to a cultivated mushroom. The cap, which averages 10cm in diameter, is white with buffish tones. The gills are white, adnate and crowded and the flesh is thick, smelling strongly of new meal. The stem is stout and white. St George's Mushroom is widespread and sometimes locally common in Europe including Britain. It prefers grassy places such as meadows and downland, and appears mainly from April to June. It is edible and good.

Nyctalis parasitica (*Asterophora parasitica*) Height up to 3cm

A small species with very specific and distinctive habitat requirements. The cap, which averages 1.5cm in diameter, is whitish with darker streaks around the margin; in its early stages, it is conical but it expands with age. The gills are whitish but appear browner with age as the spores are produced. The stem, which is relatively slender, is usually curved and is whitish in colour. The brownish flesh has a disgusting and rather putrid smell. Widespread but extremely local in occurrence. Grows on old or decaying specimens of certain *Russula* and *Lactarius* species and appears from September to November. It is not edible.

49

Porcelain Fungus *Oudemansiella mucida* Height up to 10cm

An unusual and distinctive all white fungus. The cap, which averages 6cm in diameter, is slimy and semi-translucent and best appreciated when backlit. The gills are free and widely spaced. The stem length varies considerably as it rises to clear the cap from the tree on which it grows; it is slightly scaly and carries a membranous ring. Widespread in Europe and locally common in deciduous woodland, in many regions almost exclusively on beech. It may occur on both fallen branches and high up in the tree. Appears from September to November. Although edible, it is best avoided.

Rooting Shank *Oudemansiella radicata* Height up to 12cm

A medium-sized, rather delicate looking fungus. Cap averages 7cm in diameter, is brown and radially furrowed. In its early stages the cap is conical, then it expands and may eventually have the depressed centre showing a distinct umbo. Gills are white and free, flesh is white. Tall white stem is twice the cap width, shading into brown at the base. Widespread in Europe and often common. It occurs in deciduous woodland, usually under beech, and is usually associated with buried stumps or timber. It appears from September to November and, although edible, is not really worth considering.

Velvet Shank *Flammulina velutipes* Height up to 10cm

The common English name of this species comes from the velvety texture of its stem base. Cap averages 5cm in diameter, is orange or yellow-buff, usually darker around the margins and often darkening towards the centre when wet. The gills are yellowish and the stem is orange but becoming darker towards the base; it is tough and usually curved or distorted according to the growing position of the clump. Widespread in Britain and north-western Europe. Occurs in deciduous woodland on decaying stumps of trees. Seldom appears before December. It is edible and considered good by some people.

Rhodotus palmatus Height up to 7cm

A smallish, distinctive fungus. The cap, which averages 7cm in diameter, is buffish-pink or peach-coloured with a wrinkled surface like dried fruit and a strongly inrolled margin. The gills are pale buff and the flesh is whitish. The stem, which has a fibrous appearance, is off-white, thick and often rather misshapen. Widespread in the region but its precise distribution is linked to that of its hosts, various species of elm. It is a woodland or hedgerow species which grows on dead timber and appears from September to November. It is not edible.

Fairy-ring Toadstool *Marasmius oreades* Height up to 10cm

Best known for its habit of forming often large and conspicuous rings on cultivated lawns. Cap, which averages 5cm in diameter, is pale tan; it is domed in its early stages but expands with a distinct umbo. The gills are white, adnate and widely spaced and the flesh is white. Stem is a similar colour to the cap. Like other species of this genus, it has the ability to dry out and later rehydrate without deteriorating. Widespread in Europe and grows in grassy places from August to November. Although edible, it is tough and best avoided because of confusion with similar poisonous species.

Marasmius alliaceus Height up to 15cm

A tall but delicate fungus with a powerful and distinctive smell of garlic. The cap, which averages 2.5cm in diameter, is buffish-brown to tan in colour and domed in its early stages but later becoming bell-shaped; the margin is usually streaked with radial lines. The gills are white and the flesh is whitish, becoming dark towards the base of the stem. The stem is long, thin and rich brown becoming darker towards the base. *Marasmius alliaceus* is widespread in Europe, including Britain, but seldom common. It grows among leaf litter in deciduous woodlands, often under beech, and appears from August to October. It is not edible.

A small, rather undistinguished fungus which can be easily identified by its growing habit. The cap, which averages 2cm in diameter, is buffish-tan but sometimes darker. The gills are whitish and crowded and the flesh is brownish. The stem, which is extremely slender, is usually paler than the cap and is hairy at the base. Widespread in Europe, including Britain, and locally common. This intriguing species is always found in coniferous woodland, the fungus growing from pine cones found on the forest floor. It appears from November to February and is not edible.

Spotted Tough-shank *Collybia maculata* Height up to 14cm

A medium-sized fungus with a distinctive appearance. The cap, which averages 10cm in diameter, is white or cream. The gills are white and free and the stem is white and may be elongated according to the depth of substrate in which it is growing. All parts, especially the cap and gills, develop brownish spots with age. Widespread and common in Europe including Britain. It grows in clusters in leaf litter of either deciduous or coniferous woodlands, or in bracken litter, and appears from September to November. This fungus is not edible.

Spindle-shank *Collybia fusipes* Height up to 10cm

A small to medium-sized fungus with a distinctive stem. Cap averages 6cm in diameter and is brown and smooth. Gills are fawn-coloured and free and the flesh is fawn-coloured. Stem is characteristic of the species: it is reddish-brown, longitudinally grooved and twisted, and widening and darkening towards the centre and tapering towards the base; this is often fused and forms quite a long 'root'. Widespread and often common in central and western Europe including southern Britain. Grows on oak, usually close to the base of the tree. Appears from August to October and is not edible.

Oak Tough-shank *Collybia dryophila* Height up to 5cm

An extremely common fungus which is small and variable and responsible for much of the leaf decomposition in deciduous woodland. The cap, which averages 3cm in diameter, is thin and variable in colour but usually pale. The gills are white and free and the flesh is white and thin. The stem is thin, long and hollow, widening and darkening towards the base. The Oak Tough-shank is widespread in north-western Europe including Britain. It grows in all types of woodland and also on heaths, appearing mainly from September to November. Although edible, it is not worth considering.

Greasy Tough-shank *Collybia butyracea* Height up to 8cm

A common fungus with a distinctive texture. The cap, which averages 6cm in diameter, is buffish- to olive-brown in colour. It fades as it dries, apart from the margin and umbo which results in three zones of colour. When damp, the cap has a greasy or buttery texture. The gills are whitish and the flesh is whitish with a rancid smell. Stem is pale brown, swollen at the base but tapering towards the cap. Widespread in Europe and fairly common in Britain. Grows in coniferous and deciduous woodlands. Appears from September to November. Edible but it is best avoided.

Mycena polygramma Height up to 10cm

A relatively tall but slender woodland fungus. The cap, which averages 3cm in diameter, is grey-brown or buffish-tan in colour; in its early stages it is conical but it expands and becomes bell-shaped with a slight umbo and margins that are radially streaked. Gills are off-white, sometimes flushed with pink, and are widely spaced. Flesh is whitish. The long stem is greyish in colour and often kinked at the base. Widespread in Europe including Britain and grows in deciduous woodland. It is found on stumps and buried timber, sometimes in small groups. Appears from September to November and is not edible.

Mycena inclinata Height up to 10cm

A common, clump-forming woodland fungus. The cap, which averages 2cm in diameter, is conical in its early stages but expands with age, becoming bell-shaped and bearing an umbo. It is dull orange-brown, darker towards the centre and the margins bearing radial lines, folds and tears. Gills are whitish, the flesh is whitish with a rancid smell. The stem is long, slender and brown, becoming darker towards the base. Widespread in Europe and often common in Britain. Grows in deciduous woodland, mainly on rotting stumps of oak. This fungus appears from September to November and is not edible.

Mycena galericulata Height up to 9cm

Generally a small, clump-forming species. The cap may sometimes reach 5 or 6cm in diameter and is grey but drying brownish; it is conical in its early stages but becomes flattened, usually showing a slight umbo. Gills are adnate and white, developing a flesh-pink tint with age. Flesh is white and the stem is long, thin, tough, and a similar colour to the cap. Widespread and often common in Europe, including Britain. It is a woodland species usually found growing in tufts on stumps of deciduous trees of all types. It appears from September to November and is not edible.

Mycena leptocephala Height up to 5cm

A relatively small and delicate fungus. The cap, which averages 1cm in diameter, is conical in its early stages but expands to become bell-shaped with a slight umbo; it is grey in colour with darker radial lines. Gills are paler grey than the cap, usually with a whitish margin. Whitish flesh smells of ammonia. The stem is grey and slender but usually thickens towards the base which is woolly-hairy. Widespread in Europe and locally fairly common. Its preferred habitat is short grass but it is also found among fallen leaves more occasionally. This species appears from September to November and is not edible.

Mycena epipterygia Height up to 8cm

A delicate little woodland fungus. The conical cap, which averages 1.5cm in diameter, expands and becomes bell-shaped with age; the cap colour is yellow-buff or yellow-tan, sometimes streaked around the margins, and the surface is typically very sticky. The gills are pale and the flesh is whitish. The stem is long and slender; it is slightly sticky and pale, becoming tinged with yellow towards the base. Widespread in north-western Europe including Britain. It grows in coniferous woodland among fallen pine needles and occurs on heaths and moors. Appears from August to November. Edible but not recommended.

A slender and very delicate woodland fungus. The cap, which averages 2cm in diameter, is grey-brown in colour and sometimes darker and tan towards the centre with the margin striate. It is conical in its early stages but expands and becomes bell-shaped later. Gills are whitish and crowded; flesh is whitish. Slender stem is tan coloured, and downy-hairy towards the base. Widespread in central and western Europe including Britain. It prefers deciduous or mixed woodlands where it grows attached to partly buried twigs. It appears from September to November. Edible but not recommended.

Bonnet Mycena *Mycena alcalina* Height up to 7cm

This woodland fungus is comparatively robust for its size. The cap, which averages 3cm in diameter, is conical in its early stages but expands and becomes bell-shaped with age, usually with a pronounced umbo; the cap colour is grey-brown but the umbo may be paler. The gills are widely spaced and white and the flesh is white and smells of bleach. The slender stem is grey-brown but paler than the cap. Common and widespread in Europe including Britain. Associated with coniferous woodland, it grows on stumps and partly buried timber. Appears from September to November and, although edible, is not worth considering.

Mycena crocata Height up to 8cm

A delicate and unusual species with red-staining latex. The cap, which averages 2cm in diameter, is conical in its early stages but later expands to become bell-shaped with a pronounced umbo; it is grey-brown to fawn in colour but becomes stained and blotched red with time. Gills are adnate and white, also staining red, and the flesh is whitish. The stem is slender and grey-brown, staining red. Widespread in Europe but seldom common. It is a woodland species, most typically found under beech. It appears from September to November and, although edible, is not worth considering.

Mycena fibula Height up to 4cm

A tiny and delicate fungus with a distinctive colouring. The cap, which averages 0.75cm in diameter, is rounded at first but expands to become button-shaped with a depressed centre; the cap colour is bright orange. Gills are paler than the cap and decurrent, and the flesh is orange with a mushroomy smell. The stem, which is very slender, is orange, becoming downy-hairy towards the base. Widespread in north-western Europe, including Britain, and locally common. It grows in grassy places of all kinds including lawns and appears from August to October. Although edible, this fungus is not worth considering.

Entoloma sinuatum Height up to 8cm

A sturdy, medium-sized fungus. The cap, which averages 7cm in diameter, is creamy-white to grey-buff in colour and may become waved at the margin. The gills, which are adnate, start white but become yellowish-pink as the coloured spores develop. The flesh is white and fairly thick and the stem is white and robust. Widespread in Europe including Britain although seldom particularly common. It is a species of deciduous woodland but will also occur in mature hedgerows and it appears from September to November. It is poisonous and should not be handled.

Entoloma porphyrophaeum Height up to 8cm

A rather sombre-looking, medium-sized fungus. The cap, which averages 6cm in diameter, is conical in its early stages but expands to become bell-shaped with a distinct umbo; the cap colour is buffish-brown to grey-brown and the surface is overlaid with darker, hair-like radial streaks. The gills are white at first but stain pinkish as the coloured spores develop, and the flesh is whitish. The stem is grey-brown but much paler towards the base; it has a fibrous texture. Widespread in Europe but seldom particularly common. It grows in grassy woodland rides and sometimes in pastures, and appears from June to October. Although edible, it is best avoided.

60

Nolanea cetrata (*Rhodophyllus cetratus*) Height up to 6cm

A small and rather common toadstool. The cap, which averages 2cm in diameter, is domed or umbrella-shaped in its early stages but expands and flattens later. The cap is buffish-tan to flesh-brown in colour, the centre usually appearing darker and the margins striate. The gills are pale brown and the stem, which is tall and slender, is pale brown but covered with pale silky hairs. Widespread in Britain and northern Europe but seldom numerous. This species appears in conifer woodland, often growing among Sphagnum moss, and appears from September to November. It is not edible.

Fawn Pluteus *Pluteus cervinus* Height up to 12cm

A medium-sized woodland toadstool. The cap, which averages 10cm in diameter, is varying shades of brown but usually has a darker centre with darker radial streaks; it is domed or bell-shaped at first but becomes flattened but rounded with age. The gills are whitish but acquire a pink tinge as the coloured spores develop. The flesh is white and the stem is whitish but streaked with darker fibres. Widespread in Europe including Britain and grows on stumps and sawdust from felled deciduous trees. It appears mainly from July to October and, although edible, is not worth considering.

61

Volvariella bombycina Height up to 18cm

A relatively large fungus characteristically found growing on dead wood. The cap, which averages 15cm in diameter, is domed throughout its life and has a pale buff to whitish surface covered with silky hairs that may become matted with age. The gills are whitish but become tinged with pink as the coloured spores mature. The flesh is white and the stem is white and varies greatly both in length and in curvature depending on where the specimen is growing. Widespread in Europe but only occasional in occurrence. It appears from July to October and is edible and delicious.

Cortinarius alboviolaceus Height up to 10cm

The cap of this woodland fungus averages 6cm in diameter, is whitish and usually tinged with violet; it has a silky texture and is bell-shaped in its early stages but expands to become a flattened dome. Gills are bluish but become brown as the spores mature and the flesh is bluish-white. The stem is robust and a similar colour to the cap; it has violet, fibrous lines along its length. Widespread in Britain and north-western Europe but never particularly common. Occurs in deciduous woodland and appears from September to November. Its edibility is unknown and so it should be avoided.

Cortinarius obtusus Height up to 8cm

A fungus of coniferous woodland. The cap, which averages 3cm in diameter when fully expanded, is a rich reddish-brown; in its early stages it is conical or bell-shaped but it expands and flattens with an umbo. The gills and flesh are orange-brown. Stem is brown but appears white due to a coating of fibres; it is of uniform width along its length although it may taper towards the base. Widespread in Europe including Britain but only occasional in occurrence. It grows mainly under pines and appears from July to October. Its edibility is unknown and so it should be avoided.

Cortinarius pseudosalor Height up to 10cm

The commonest of several similar *Cortinarius* species that are difficult to distinguish in the field. The cap, 8cm in diameter when fully expanded, is rich brown and slimy, paler and striate on the outer third; rounded at first, expanding and flattening with age. Gills are adnate and rusty coloured; flesh is pale brown. The stem is slimy and slightly swollen in the middle; it is pale blue and shows a darker ring zone where the cap edge separated from it. Widespread in central and western Europe including Britain. It grows mainly in deciduous woodland. It appears from July to November and is not edible.

Cortinarius torvus Height up to 6cm

An easily overlooked fungus. The cap, which averages 7cm in diameter when fully expanded, is rounded at first but expands and flattens with age, still retaining its rounded profile; the cap colour is buffish-tan and there are darker, radiating fibres on the surface. Grey-brown gills become stained darker as the coloured spores mature. Flesh is bluish-white and the stem is whitish and has a ring, above which the stem is darker. Widespread but seldom common. It grows in deciduous woodland, especially under beech, and appears from September to November. Its edibility is unknown and it should therefore be avoided.

Cortinarius bolaris Height up to 5cm

The cap of this attractive fungus, which averages 4cm in diameter, has a pale, buffish ground colour but the surface is covered with a mosaic of reddish scales; the cap is domed throughout its life but is broadly flattened when mature. Gills are pale buff at first but become stained darker as the spores mature. The flesh is whitish in the cap and yellowish towards the base of the stem, the colour intensifying with exposure to air. Robust, pale stem is covered with dark red scales. Widespread but seldom numerous. It grows in deciduous woodlands and appears from August to October. It is poisonous.

Cortinarius uliginosus Height up to 6cm

A distinctively colourful toadstool. The cap, which averages 3cm in diameter, is rounded or globular in its early stages but expands with age; it is bright orange-brown in colour with a slightly fibrous texture. Gills are yellowish, becoming darker as the spores mature. The flesh is yellow and the stem is a similar colour to the cap although slightly paler and covered with fibres. Widespread but never numerous. It grows in damp ground, sometimes in damp alder carr woodland or on boggy heaths. It appears from September to November and is probably not edible.

Cortinarius semisanguineus Height up to 8cm

The cap of this rather attractive fungus, which averages 4cm in diameter when fully expanded, is rounded or conical in its early stages but expands and develops a pronounced umbo; it is orange-buff in colour. The gills are deep red and contrast markedly with the cap. Flesh is orange-buff as is the stem although it is paler than the cap colour; its shape is often slightly distorted. Widespread in Europe, including Britain, and locally common. It is most usually encountered in mixed woodlands with pines and birches and appears from September to November. It is probably not edible.

Poison Pie *Hebeloma crustuliniforme* Height up to 7cm

As its name suggests, a poisonous fungus. Cap, which averages 4cm in diameter, is pale tan but darkening in the centre almost to a dark brick colour; it is sticky and remains inrolled at the margins for a long time. Clay coloured gills eventually become brown as the spores mature; they are adnate and, in wet weather, develop drops of water on the edges, which catch the spores and dry to leave brown spots. The flesh is white and thick and the stem is pale whitish-fawn. Widespread in north-western Europe including Britain. It grows in deciduous woodlands and appears from September to November. It is definitely not edible.

Inocybe maculata Height up to 9cm

A small to medium-sized fungus. The cap, which averages 6cm in diameter when fully expanded, is pale brown but generously covered with dark brown, radial streaks and fibrous hairs; in its early stages it is conical but it later becomes flattened with an umbo. Whitish gills darken as the spores mature. White flesh has a strong smell. Stem is brown, paler than the cap, with varying amounts of streaking along its length. Widespread in central and western Europe including Britain. It grows in deciduous woodland, often under beech, and appears from September to November. It is poisonous and should be avoided.

Red-staining Inocybe *Inocybe patouillardii*
Height up to 10cm

This species sometimes forms distinct rings. The cap, which averages 6cm in diameter, is white or pinkish white; it is rounded or conical in its early stages but expands and flattens with an umbo and a margin that often splits. The gills are whitish but become darker as the spores mature. The stem is whitish. All parts of the fungus stain red with age. Widespread in Europe including Britain. It grows in deciduous woodland, especially on chalk soils under beech, and appears from June to November. This species is extremely poisonous and should not be handled.

Inocybe dulcamara Height up to 4cm

A small fungus most usually associated with very bare situations. The cap, which averages 2.5cm in diameter, is pale brown to tan in colour and is coated with felt-like hairs; in its early stages it is conical but it expands and flattens with age. The gills are adnate and yellow-buff, staining darker with age. The flesh is buffish and the the stem is the same colour as the cap. Widespread in north-western Europe, including Britain, but never numerous. It favours loose soils and will even grow on sand dunes, appearing from August to October. It is not edible.

67

Inocybe fastigiata Height up to 6cm

A small to medium-sized woodland fungus. The cap, which averages 4cm in diameter, is reminiscent of a bell-tent in shape in its early stages; it later expands and flattens. The cap colour is pale yellowish and the surface characteristically splits radially revealing the pale flesh underneath. The gills are dirty yellow with a white edge; they are crowded and adnate. The stem is even, fairly tall and slim and a similar colour to the cap. Widespread in Europe including Britain. It grows under deciduous trees, especially beech, and appears from July to October. It is poisonous and best avoided.

Inocybe napipes Height up to 6cm

A small and rather undistinguished woodland fungus. The cap, which averages 3.5cm in diameter, is conical in its early stages but expands to become bell-shaped with a distinct umbo; the colour is rich brown and the surface is covered with radial fibrous hairs. The gills are brown and the flesh is whitish. The stem expands towards the bulbous base and is buffish in colour. Widespread and often common in north-western Europe including Britain. It grows mainly in deciduous woodlands, but also in mixed settings, and appears from August to October. It is a poisonous fungus.

Inocybe godeyi Height up to 6cm

One of several similar *Inocybe* species with rather fibrous caps. The cap, which averages 3cm in diameter, is orange-brown with a fibrous appearance; there are dark radial streaks and the margins are often split. Conical at first, it expands and becomes broad later with an umbo. The gills are whitish but acquire a brownish hue with age. Flesh is white, stem is grey-brown with a bulbous base; like the cap, it bruises red. Widespread but never numerous in Europe including Britain. It grows in woodlands on chalk, especially under beech, and appears from September to November. It is poisonous and best avoided.

Inocybe geophylla var. *lilaciana* Height up to 5cm

A striking and attractive little fungus. The cap, which averages 2cm in diameter, is conical in its early stages but expands with age, acquiring a distinct umbo; the cap colour is pale lilac and the surface is smooth. The gills are grey-brown but darken with age. The flesh is lilac and the stem is even, fairly long relative to the cap and often bent. The species also occurs as *Inocybe geophylla*, a white form where the lilac hue is absent. The species is widespread in Europe, including Britain, and appears from August to October. It grows in wooded habitats and is a poisonous fungus.

Gymnopilus penetrans Height up to 7cm

A common, small to medium-sized fungus. The cap, which averages 5cm in diameter, is conical in its early stages but expands and becomes flattened without an umbo; the cap colour is orange-brown and the surface is smooth. The gills are orange-brown at first but become stained darker as the spores mature. The flesh is yellowish and the stem is yellowish, darkening towards the base. Widespread in Europe including Britain. It occurs in coniferous woodland, growing on fallen, and sometimes buried, branches and timber, and appears from August to November. It is not edible.

Gymnopilus junonius Height up to 12cm

An often large, tufted species. The cap, which averages 12cm in diameter, is deep golden yellow and the surface is covered with scales forming streaks or patches; it is rounded at first but expands and flattens with age. The gills are adnate, yellow and coloured by rusty spores which fall on the stem. Flesh is yellow and the stem is coloured as the cap; it is stout and swollen towards the base. Widespread in Europe including Britain. Often grows on buried deciduous wood, so the fungus appears to grow on the ground. It appears from August to November and is not edible.

Two-toned Pholiote *Galerina (Kuehneromyces) mutabilis*
Height up to 8cm

The patterned cap, which averages 5cm in diameter, is brown and recognised by the fact that it changes colour as it dries, becoming pale in the centre; conical at first, the cap soon expands and flattens with a slight umbo. The gills are pale cinnamon-brown and adnate and the flesh is whitish-cinnamon. The stem is smooth and pale above the ring but dark and scaly below. Widespread in Europe including Britain. It grows in clumps on deciduous wood and appears from July to November. Although edible, it should be avoided due to potential confusion with dangerous species.

Galerina mycenopsis (*Galerina pumila*) Height up to 6cm

The cap of this unobtrusive fungus, which averages 1cm in diameter, is rounded in its early stages but expands to become bell-shaped with age; the cap colour is orange-brown and it may appear slightly darker towards the centre. Gills are yellowish-brown and the flesh is similar in colour. The stem, which is relatively long and slender, is yellowish-brown, paler than the cap, and often expands towards the base. Widespread in Europe, including Britain, but seldom numerous. It grows in mossy places such as lawns and grassland and appears from August to November. It is best avoided.

71

Stropharia hornemanni Height up to 12cm

The cap of this distinctive fungus, which averages 12cm in diameter, is globular but later expands to become broadly domed; the cap colour is buffish-tan, often with a violet hue, and the surface is sticky when wet. Gills are greyish with a violet hue. Whitish flesh has a strong, unpleasant smell. The stem, which may be curved due to the growing position, is white and scaly below the ring. Widespread in north-western Europe, including Britain, but usually rather local. It is a woodland species growing on rotting stumps and buried timber. It appears from September to November and is not edible.

Dung Roundhead *Stropharia semiglobata* Height up to 10cm

This extremely common species grows, as its name suggests, on dung. The cap, which averages 3cm in diameter, is pale yellow and hemispherical. The gills are black and widely spaced; they form a flat plane between the cap margin and the stem to which they are attached, adding to the hemispherical appearance of the cap. The stem is of a similar colour to the cap and carries a slight black ring, below which the stem is sticky. This species is widespread in Europe including Britain. It especially grows on horse dung and appears from June to November. This species is not edible.

Sulphur Tuft *Hypholoma fasciculare* Height up to 8cm

This species invariably forms large clumps. Cap, averaging 5cm in diameter, is sulphur-yellow when young with a slightly darker disc. Yellow gills develop a green tint and then blacken with age; they are adnate. The flesh is yellowish and the stem is the same colour as the cap; it is usually curved or twisted depending on the growing position of the specimen. Widespread in Europe including Britain. It grows in tufts of up to 100, the lower caps becoming discoloured by the black spores of those above. Found on dead wood and appears from June to December. This species is not edible.

Hypholoma marginatum Height up to 7cm

This fungus could easily be mistaken for the Sulphur Tuft or Brick Caps were it not for its habitat preference. The cap, averaging 3cm in diameter, is orange-brown or tan coloured, usually with the margin slightly paler; it is conical or rounded when young but flattening with age. The gills are yellowish but turn brown with age and the flesh is pale buff, darkening towards the base of the stem. The stem is orange-brown and silky-hairy. Widespread in Europe, including Britain, but rather local. It grows in coniferous woodland and appears from August to November. It is not edible.

73

Brick Caps *Hypholoma sublateritium* Height up to 15cm

A small to medium-sized fungus. The cap, which averages 7cm in diameter, is rounded at first but expands and flattens with age. As its common English name suggests, the cap colour is often brick-red, although it can be orange-tan; the margin is usually paler. The gills are pale at first but darken with age and the flesh is yellow-brown. The tough stem is brown and darkens towards the base. Widespread and locally common in Europe including Britain. It grows in clumps on the rotting stumps of deciduous trees and appears from October to December. It is not edible.

Liberty Cap *Psilocybe semilanceata* Height up to 6cm

A small species whose hallucinogenic properties have earned it the nickname 'Magic Mushroom'. The cap, which averages 1cm in diameter, is characteristically bonnet-shaped with a pointed tip and an incurved margin; it is covered with a glutinous pellicle and is olive-brown in colour. The gills are black and adnate and the stem is long, thin and pale buff in colour. Widespread and locally common in most of Europe including Britain. It grows in short grassy places of all kinds and appears from June to November. Its hallucinogenic properties mean that it should not be eaten.

The cap of this species, which averages 9cm in diameter, is bright orange-brown and covered with dark, fibrous scales, appearing especially dark in the centre; it is domed at first but expands and flattens with age. The gills are yellow-brown but darken with age and the flesh is pale, becoming darker towards the stem base. The stem is yellow brown and smooth above the ring but scaly below. Widespread in Europe and seldom numerous. It grows in clusters on stumps of deciduous trees, especially beech, and appears from July to November. It is not edible.

Shaggy Pholiota *Pholiota squarrosa* Height up to 12cm

The cap of this tufted species, which averages 8cm in diameter, is deep yellow and covered in dark brown scales. In its early stages, the cap is domed but it later expands and flattens. The gills are adnate and yellow, shedding rusty brown spores. The stem is long in relation to the size of the cap and has a ground colour and scales to match the cap. Common and widespread in Europe including Britain. It grows in clumps at the base of deciduous trees, often on beech, and appears from September to November. It is not edible.

Pholiota cerifera (Pholiota aurivella) Height up to 10cm

This species is superficially similar to the Shaggy Pholiota. The cap, which averages 10cm in diameter, is orange-brown with fewer, larger dark scales than other *Pholiota* species, these often absent from the centre; in its early stages the cap is domed but with time it flattens and expands. The gills are yellow and shed rusty brown spores. The stem is fibrous and the same colour as the cap; it is often curved, depending on the growing position. Widespread in Europe including southern Britain. Grows on the stumps of deciduous trees. Appears from September to November. It is not edible.

Bolbitius vitellinus Height up to 6cm

A small to medium-sized grassland species. The cap, which averages 4cm in diameter, is bell-shaped and creamy-white, developing a yellow centre; at first it is viscid but later becomes furrowed and splits at the margin. The gills are adnate and yellowish at first, becoming rusty with time. The stem is tall and slim and tends to thicken at the base; it is creamy and at first is covered with a pale meal. Widespread in Europe including Britain. This species grows on dung or in dung-enriched meadows and appears from July to November. It is not an edible species.

Agrocybe cylindracea (*Agrocybe aegerita*) Height up to 10cm

A medium-sized species. The cap, which averages 7cm in diameter, is broadly rounded in its early stages but becomes flattened with age, the margin often wavy and tattered. The gills are adnate and pale at first but become darker as the spores mature. The stem is pale, darkening with age and bearing a ring. Widespread in north-western Europe, including Britain, but never numerous. It is rather particular in its requirements, growing almost exclusively on willow and poplar, usually forming small clumps. It can be seen in most months of the year and is edible.

Agrocybe praecox Height up to 7cm

A small to medium-sized fungus. The cap, which averages 5cm in diameter, is buffish-tan darkening towards the centre and often with a narrow, dark margin; in its early stages it is broadly rounded but it expands with age. The gills are adnate and pinkish-brown, darkening as the spores mature. The stem is pale and has a ring. Widespread but rather uncommon in most parts of north-western Europe including Britain. It favours grassy, often overgrown places such as woodland rides, and appears from July to October. This species is edible.

Brown Hay Cap *Panaeolus foenisecii* Height up to 6cm

A small and distinctive grassland species. The cap, which averages 2cm in diameter, is typically bell-shaped or rounded-conical; the margins sometimes tear and the cap colour is brown although, when it dries, the centre may appear paler. The gills are pale brown but become stained and mottled darker with age. The stem is slender and brown but paler than the cap. Common and widespread in many parts of northern Europe including Britain. It grows in all sorts of habitats with short grass including lawns and parks, and appears from July to November. It is not edible.

Dung Fungus *Panaeolus semiovatus* Height up to 10cm

A dung-loving species that can vary considerably in size from small to medium. The cap, which averages 4cm in diameter, is pale creamy-buff; it is the shape of half an oval as its scientific name implies. The gills are adnate, black and unevenly spotted and the flesh is pale and slight. The stem is the same colour as the cap and bears a black fibrous ring half way down; it is tall and slim. The Dung Fungus is widespread in central and northern Europe including Britain. This intriguing species grows in horse dung and appears from July to November. It is not edible.

Panaeolus sphinctrinus Height up to 10cm

This species undergoes an extreme change in colour as it dries. The cap, which averages 3cm in diameter, is blackish-brown when young but changes to pale creamy-ochre, darker in the centre; it is bell-shaped and the margin has a frill of white fibres when fresh. The gills are black and adnate. The stem also changes colour as it dries from dark brown to cream at the apex. Widespread in northern and north-western Europe including Britain. It usually grows in dung-enriched grassland, and appears almost throughout the year. This species is not edible.

Panaeolus campanulatus Height up to 10cm

The cap of this delicate fungus, which averages 3cm in diameter, is hemispherical, or more accurately hemi-ovate in outline. It is buffish-brown in colour, becoming darker tan towards the cap centre and the surface is slightly sticky in damp weather. Gills are adnate and grey-brown, becoming black as the spores mature. The stem is relatively tall and slender and grey-brown in colour; the base may appear twisted or distorted depending on the growing position. Widespread in Europe but seldom numerous. It grows in nutrient-rich grassland and appears from August to October. It is not edible.

79

A slender, delicate fungus. The cap, which averages 2cm in diameter, is rich brown in damp weather but dries grey-buff, sometimes with the margin appearing darker; it is domed at first but expands, becoming bell-shaped with age. Reddish-brown gills become darker as the spores mature. The stem is tall, extremely slender and pale buff in colour; it is easily broken. Common and widespread in central and western Europe including Britain. It grows in open places such as pathsides and bare ground and appears from September to November. It is not edible.

Crumble Tuft *Psathyrella candolleana* Height up to 8cm

A rather fragile fungus. The cap, which averages 5cm in diameter, is domed and rounded in its early stages but expands to become flattened-conical in outline. The cap colour is pale buffish-brown and there may be striations on the margin; the cap splits and breaks readily. The gills are greyish-lilac but darken as the spores mature. The stem is brittle and hollow. Common and widespread in Europe including Britain. It grows in all sorts of wayside places such as hedgerows and woodland rides, appearing from July to November. It is not edible.

Psathyrella hydrophila Height up to 10cm

The cap of this clump-forming species, which averages 3cm in diameter, is brown but as the fungus ages and dries the centre fades to buffish-tan; the cap is broadly rounded. The gills are crowded and pale brown but darken as the spores mature. The stem is whitish but darkening towards the base which is often curved or distorted depending on the growing position. Common and widespread in Europe including Britain. It grows in gardens, hedgerows and woodland rides, usually beside rotting tree stumps, and appears from July to October. It is not edible.

Psathyrella obtusata Height up to 7cm

A small fungus which, although it looks robust, is rather fragile. The cap, which averages 2cm in diameter, is domed in its early stages but flattens and expands with age; it is buffish-brown when damp but dries paler, the centre often remaining a rich brown colour. The gills are pale brown at first but become darker as the spores mature. The stem is pale and hollow. Widespread in central and western Europe including Britain. It is a woodland species usually seen growing on bare ground and appears from June to October. This fungus is not edible.

81

Weeping Widow *Lacrymaria velutina (Psathyrella lacryma-bunda)* Height up to 8cm

The cap of this species, which averages 8cm in diameter, is pale ochre-brown and convex; it is covered with woolly fibrils which overhang the edge as a fringe. The gills are adnate and dark purplish-brown with a white edge; they are characteristically covered in droplets, hence the common English name. The stem is white at the top, but becoming brown below the ring-zone; it is scaly towards the base. Widespread in Europe including Britain. It is found on grassy roadsides and tracks and appears from June to October. Although edible, the taste is not altogether pleasant.

Coprinus niveus Height up to 6cm

This fungus has a distinctive habitat preference. The cap, which averages 3cm in diameter, is slender-conical or thimble-shaped in its early stages but later expands and flattens, the margin rolling back and blackening with age; the cap is whitish with a powdery surface, as is covered with chalk dust. The gills are white at first Widespread in Europe including Britain and fairly common in suitable habitats. It grows on horse or cow dung and appears from July to November. Its edibility is unknown and so it should be avoided.

Coprinus silvaticus Height up to 8cm

A small and compact fungus. The cap, which averages 1cm in diameter and 2cm in height, is olive-buff and marked with dark, radial lines which are most conspicuous towards the margin; the centre is usually darker and the cap is usually thimble-shaped. The gills are whitish at first but blacken as the spores mature. The stem is whitish but becomes buffish-brown towards the base. Widespread but local in north-western Europe, including Britain, and usually scarce. It grows in small clumps on buried, rotting timber and appears from September to November. It is probably not edible.

Coprinus plicatilis Height up to 7cm

This species changes shape and colour markedly throughout its life. The cap, which averages 1cm high in its early stages and 1.5cm in diameter when expanded, is thimble-shaped and buffish when young with a darker centre. It later expands and flattens, sometimes with a depressed centre, and becomes greyish with a grooved and marked margin. Pinkish gills blacken as the spores mature. The stem is whitish becoming brownish towards the base. Widespread in north-western Europe including Britain. It grows on lawns and paths and appears from June to October. Although edible, it is not worth considering.

Glistening Ink Cap *Coprinus micaceus* Height up to 9cm

This species forms clumps. The cap, which averages 4cm in diameter, is pale ochre-yellow, becoming darker towards the centre and ornamented on the top with glistening flecks of veil; it soon darkens with age and loses the micaceous granules. Oval at first, it becomes bell-shaped with age. The gills are free and white when young but blacken with age, and the flesh is whitish-grey. The stem is white and smooth. Common and widespread in northern and western Europe including Britain. It grows on wood, in dense clusters. Appears from July to November and, although edible, is not particularly good.

Magpie Ink Cap *Coprinus picaceus* Height up to 25cm

The cap of this distinctive species is thimble-shaped and averages 6cm in height in its early stages and later expands to an average diameter of 7cm. It is pale grey-brown when young but later darkens as the fungus ages with small patches of pale veil adhering. Pinkish gills darken as the spores mature and eventually liquefy. The stem is white with a bulbous, downy base. Widespread but rather local species in Britain and Europe. It is a woodland species and is usually found growing under beech on chalky soils. Appears from August to September. It is poisonous.

Coprinus lagopus Height up to 12cm

An unobtrusive woodland fungus. The cap is almost cylindrical in its early stages, an average of 3cm long and pale greyish but covered with a white dusting of veil remains. In time the cap expands and flattens to an average diameter of 4cm, the surface becoming grey and radially striated. The gills are pale but soon turn black and the stem is white with a bulbous base. Widespread in Britain and north-western Europe but seldom numerous. It grows mainly in deciduous woodland and appears from August to October. Although edible, it is not worth considering.

Common Ink Cap *Coprinus atramentarius*
Height up to 16cm

A medium-sized species which is normally tufted. The cap, which averages 7cm in diameter, is greyish-white but soon turns black; it is egg-shaped and furrowed and fails to open fully. The gills are free and white, becoming black and liquefying into 'ink', which was once used for writing. The stem is tall and fairly slim. Widespread in Britain and Europe. It grows in woodland rides, lawns and paths and appears from July to November. Although edible, it contains a chemical related to 'Antabuse' which will cause sickness if eaten in conjunction with alcohol.

Fairies' Bonnets *Coprinus disseminatus* Height up to 4cm

A small fungus which grows in large clumps of up to fifty. The cap is thimble-shaped and averages 1cm in length when young; the surface is greyish-buff and deeply furrowed. With age, the cap expands. The gills are whitish but soon darken as the spores mature; they do not, however, liquefy. The stem is almost hidden by the cap and is whitish and downy. Common and widespread in central and western Europe including southern parts of Britain. It grows on the rotting stumps of deciduous trees and appears from August to November. It is not worth eating.

Shaggy Ink Cap *Coprinus comatus* Height up to 30cm

This familiar fungus is also known as Lawyer's Wig. The cap averages 8cm in length, is white but becomes brown on top; it is oval and hairy-scaly, the hairs turning outwards at an intermediate stage. The gills are pinkish and free but become black with spores and liquefy so that the spores are spread by rain. Flesh is white when young, the stem is tall and white when young. Widespread in Britain and Europe. It grows in grassy places and appears from August to October. It is edible and good but only so before the gills have started to liquefy.

Yellow Staining Mushroom *Agaricus xanthodermus*
Height up to 15cm

This inedible species may be mistaken for an edible mushroom. The cap, which averages 10cm in diameter, is white and similar in shape to the cultivated mushroom; it stains bright yellow when bruised. Whitish to pale pink gills become grey, then black; they are adnate to free. The flesh at the base of the stem discolours yellow when it is cut and has an unpleasant smell. The stem has a ring. Widespread in Britain and Europe. Grows in cultivated fields and grassy places, appearing from July to November. It can cause quite severe digestive disturbances so should not be eaten.

Brown Wood Mushroom *Agaricus silvaticus*
Height up to 10cm

The cap of this distinctive fungus, which averages 8cm when fully expanded, is broadly rounded and pale brown, this ground colour almost hidden by brown scaly fibres that resemble matted hair. Pinkish gills darken with age. The flesh turns red when cut or bruised and the stem is whitish and covered with coarse scales below the ring. Widespread in Britain and northern Europe and locally common. It grows in coniferous woodland and occasionally in mixed woodland, appearing from September to November. Edible and good.

Wood Mushroom *Agaricus silvicola* Height up to 9cm

The cap of this woodland species averages 9cm in diameter, is yellowish-white, smooth and shining; it is rounded in its early stages but expands and flattens with age. The gills are adnate and greyish-pink becoming dark brown with age. The stem is the same colour as the cap and has a slightly bulbous base and carries a large ring. The flesh is thin and the fungus smells of aniseed when fresh. Widespread in Britain and northern Europe. It favours both deciduous and coniferous woodland and appears from September to November. It is edible and good.

The Prince *Agaricus augustus* Height up to 20cm

The cap of this striking fungus averages 15cm in diameter, is rounded in its early stages but expands and flattens with age; the surface is buffish-brown but is covered with numerous smallish dark brown scales, the colouring most intense towards the centre. Whitish gills become brown with age. The flesh tastes mushroomy and the stem is whitish with scales below the ring. Found in Britain, where it is rather scarce, and across western and central Europe, where it is more common. It grows in both coniferous and deciduous woodland and appears from August to October. It is edible and good.

Parasol Mushroom *Lepiota procera* (*Macrolepiota procera*)
Height up to 30cm

The cap of this rather impressive fungus can measure up to 25cm in diameter. It is buff with brown scales, egg-shaped in its early stages but parasol-shaped with a central umbo when expanded. Gills are white and free. The stem is brownish and covered with a darker layer which breaks up into snake-like markings; it carries a double ring which sits high up the stem but may be moved up and down as it has no attachment. Common and widespread in Britain and Europe. It grows in grassy places and appears from July to November. It is edible and delicious.

Stinking Parasol *Lepiota cristata* Height up to 4cm

As its name suggests this species has an unpleasant smell. Cap has distinct markings; it averages 4cm in diameter, is pale-buff to off-white with a dark reddish-brown central umbo and similarly coloured scales arranged in irregular zones on the surface, sometimes appearing in loose concentric rings. The gills are white and free and the flesh smells of tar when crushed. The stem is grey-buff and slender with a ring. Widespread but seldom common in Britain and Europe. It grows along woodland rides and in hedgerows, appearing from August to November. It is inedible and may be poisonous.

Shaggy Parasol *Macrolepiota rhacodes* Height up to 15cm

A large and impressive fungus. The cap, which can measure up to 25cm in diameter when fully expanded, is pale buff with shaggy, pale brown scales; it is egg-shaped at first but expands and becomes parasol-shaped with a shallow umbo. The gills are white and free and the flesh is white. The stem is brownish and unmarked; it carries a double ring which sits high up the stem. Common and widespread in Britain and Europe. It grows in grassy woodland rides and overgrown hedgerows, appearing from July to November. It is edible and delicious.

Lepiota friesii Height up to 8cm

The cap of this woodland parasol averages 7cm in diameter when fully expanded and is egg-shaped to bell-shaped in its early stages. Cap surface has a pale- to rich-brown ground colour and is covered with dark brown scales, the centre appearing particularly dark. Gills are white and free and the flesh is white. The stem is brown and bears a conspicuous ring above which the colour is paler; the base is normally swollen. Widespread in Britain and north-western Europe but seldom numerous. It grows in deciduous woodlands and occurs from September to November. It is probably not edible.

Amanita solitaria Height up to 12cm

The broadly domed to flattened cap of this unusual toadstool averages 12cm. It is whitish to pale grey-buff and covered with large, felty scales, some of which overlap the cap margin. Gills are white and free and the flesh is white. The stem is white and stout with a ring and a bulbous base enclosed in the remains of the volva; the surface is covered in shaggy, felty scales. Widespread but local in central and western Europe but distinctly rare in Britain. Grows near woodland on chalk-rich soil. Appears from August to October. Edible but may be confused with poisonous species.

Panther Cap *Amanita pantherina* Height up to 11cm

An attractive and distinctive toadstool. The cap, which averages 7cm in diameter, is brown and covered with white patches which are the remains of the volva; the cap is almost round at first but expands and flattens. The gills are white and free. The flesh and stem are white and the stem does not turn pink when damaged. This species is locally common and widespread in Britain and Europe. It grows in deciduous woodland, most often under beech, and appears from August to November. The species is highly poisonous and can be fatal although it is not as toxic as some of its more deadly relatives.

Death Cap *Amanita phalloides* Height up to 12cm

As its name suggests, one of the most poisonous toadstools in the region - eating only one cap can cause death. It has a sickly sweet smell. The cap, which averages 7cm in diameter, is whitish but darkened centrally by radiating fibres of green or sometimes yellow. Gills are free and white and flesh is white. White stem usually has a ring but often the veil which forms the ring remains hanging on the cap edge instead; the base of the stem is surrounded by a marked volva. Widespread in Europe but rather local in Britain. It occurs in woodland, usually under oak, and appears from September to November. Do not even touch this species.

False Death Cap *Amanita citrina* Height up to 7cm

Superficially similar to the Death Cap. Cap averages 6cm in diameter, is lemon-coloured with large white patches. The gills are white and almost free and the flesh is white. The stem is fairly tall and has a ring; it is swollen into a large bulb at the base and this is enclosed in the remains of the volva. All parts of the fungus have a strong smell of raw potatoes, particularly when cut. Common and widespread in Britain and Europe. It grows in many types of woodland and appears from August to November. It is inedible.

The Blusher *Amanita rubescens* Height up to 15cm

The pink colour of the stem gives this fungus its common name. Cap averages 8-10cm in diameter, is pale brown and covered with grey patches formed from the remains of the veil. Gills are white and free, the flesh is white. White stem turns pink and has a ring which, on its outer surface, shows striations formed from contact with the gills. Stem broadens towards the base where it is ridged by remains of the bottom part of the volva. Widespread and often common in Britain and Europe. Grows in woodland from August to October. Edible but may be confused with the poisonous Panther Cap.

Fly Agaric *Amanita muscaria* Height up to 18cm

The quintessential toadstool, named for its former use as a preparation for killing flies. The cap, which averages 8cm in diameter, is brilliant red and usually covered with white spots and flecks, the remains of the veil; the white spots may be lost after heavy rain and the colour also washes out of the cap, leaving it orange. The gills are white and free and the stem is white, with a ring. Common and widespread in Britain and northern and central Europe. Grows in association with birch in woodland and heath and appears from August to November. It is poisonous.

Amanita excelsa (Amanita spissa) Height up to 12cm

Superficially similar to the Panther Cap or the Blusher. The cap, which averages 9cm in diameter, is greyish-brown and covered by large patches of greyish-white flecks, the remains of the veil; these are lost in heavy rain. The gills and flesh are white and the flesh does not bruise pink. The stem is pale brown with a bulbous base and a paler, striated ring. Widespread and often common in Britain and Europe. It grows in woodland of all kinds and appears from August to November. Although possibly edible, it should be avoided due to potential confusion with dangerous species.

Amanita aspera Height up to 10cm

A distinctly local toadstool. The cap, which averages 8cm in diameter when fully expanded, starts off as egg-shaped or domed but expands and flattens; it is yellow buff in colour and covered with dirty yellowish scales, the remains of the veil. The gills are adnate and white and the flesh is white but discolouring where damaged by slugs. The stem is robust and has a bulbous base enclosed in a volva. Widespread but local in Europe but rather rare in Britain. It grows in deciduous woodlands and appears from September to November. It is not edible.

Tawny Grisette *Amanita fulva* Height up to 12cm

One of the comparatively few harmless *Amanita* species. The cap, which averages 5-8cm in diameter, is tawny with marked striations radially placed all round the outer margin. The gills and flesh are white. The stem is relatively tall but with no ring, and has a large and conspicuous volva. Widespread and locally common in Britain and Europe. It occurs in deciduous woodlands, often under oak, and appears from August to November. Although edible, it is perhaps best avoided because of possible confusion with its poisonous relatives.

Grisette *Amanita vaginata* Height up to 15cm

Superficially very similar to the Tawny Grisette. The cap, averages 8cm in diameter, is rounded in its early stages but becomes flattened with age; it is grey-brown and marked with radial striations all round the margin. Gills and flesh are white. Pale brown stem is slender, the base enclosed in a volva, and does not have a ring. Widespread and sometimes common in Britain and Europe. Grows in deciduous woodland and appears from September to November. Although edible, it is best avoided because of confusion with poisonous relatives.

Amanita inaurata (Amanitopsis strangulata)
Height up to 12cm

The cap of this toadstool, which averages 10cm when fully expanded, starts off rounded but becomes flattened; it is orange-brown and is covered with large, flaky, grey-brown coloured patches, the remains of the veil, which are most concentrated towards the centre. The cap margin is usually pale and shows radial striations. The gills and flesh are white. The stem is dirty greyish-white with fibrous hairs and the base is enclosed in a volva. Local and generally scarce in Britain and Europe. It grows in woodland and appears from September to November. It is probably not edible.

Stinkhorn *Phallus impudicus* Height up to 15cm

This striking and unmistakable fungus starts as a soft whitish ball about 4-6cm in diameter and full of a jelly-like mass. When mature, the case splits and in the course of a few hours the fruit body rises out of the volva. It consists of a fragile, white phallus-shaped structure, capped by an oval mass of brownish-green mucus containing the spores. This has a characteristic sickly smell which attracts flies. Common and widespread in Britain and Europe. Grows mainly in deciduous woodland and can appear at any time of year from May to November. It is not edible.

Phallus hadrianii Height up to 12cm

Superficially very similar to the closely related Stinkhorn. The fungus starts as a soft whitish ball about 3-5cm in diameter and full of a jelly-like mass. When mature, the case splits and the phallus-like fruit body emerges from it over the course of a few hours; it is capped by an oval mass of greenish-brown mucus, smaller in size than that of the Stinkhorn, which attracts flies to assist in spore dispersal. Local and rather uncommon in Britain and Europe being restricted to stabilised coastal sand-dunes. It appears from July to October and is not edible.

Dog Stinkhorn *Mutinus caninus* Height up to 10cm

A strange fungus, similar in its growth habits to the Stinkhorn. It starts as an 'egg' which is about 2cm in diameter and located on the ground among leaf litter. From this a long, slender fruit body emerges which is capped with greenish mucus; the stem has a slightly orange tint and, once the gluten is removed, the tip is quite a bright orange. Widespread in Britain and Europe but seldom particularly numerous. It grows in deciduous woodland, appearing from August to November. Excavation near fruitbody will probably reveal other 'eggs'. It is not edible.

Common Bird's-nest Fungus *Crucibulum vulgare (C.laeve)*
Height up to 7mm

This fungus bears a fanciful resemblence to a bird's nest. When mature, the fruit body forms a neat bowl with a smooth yellowish-grey inner surface and an outer surface covered with fibrous hairs. Inside the cup are 10 or more whitish and flattened 'eggs', the capsules that contain the spores. These are attached to the cup by filaments which, when the spores are ripe, are broken as raindrops hit the cup and bounce the eggs out. Widespread in Britain and Europe but rather local. It grows on dead wood and appears in September and October. It is not edible.

Bird's-nest Fungus *Cyathus striatus* Height up to 1cm

The fruit body of this fungus resembles a bird's nest. When mature, it averages 0.75cm in diameter. It forms a cone-shaped bowl, the inner surface of which is smooth, greyish-white and radially grooved; the outer surface is covered with coarse, fibrous hairs. Inside the cup there are several whitish, flattened 'eggs', attached to the cup base with thin filaments. Heavy drops of rain bounce the eggs out of the cup, breaking the filaments. Widespread in Britain and Europe but local. It grows on dead wood and appears from September to November. It is not edible.

Cyathus olla Height up to 15cm

A bird's-nest fungus which is superficially similar in appearance, but not habitat preferences, to its relatives. When mature, the fruit body is an average of 10mm in diameter and is conical in shape, the margin being rolled back like the rim of a vase. In the bottom of the cup are several greyish, flattened 'eggs' containing the spores; these are attached to the cup by threads which break when heavy raindrops bounce the eggs out. Widespread in Britain and Europe but often overlooked. It grows mainly on bare soil and appears from April to November. Inedible.

Common Earth-ball *Scleroderma citrinum* (*S. auranticum*)
Width up to 10cm

This common and distinctive fungus resembles an old, cracked tennis ball. The fruit body is roughly globose and has a thick skin which is dark ochre-brown on the outside and is covered with coarse, flaky scales. As the fungus matures, it expands and the surface splits, showing more and more of the yellow inner layer. The centre comprises a black spore mass. There is no opening for spore discharge and the fungus splits irregularly. Widespread in Britain and Europe. It grows in woodland and appears from August to November. Inedible.

Earth Star *Geastrum triplex* Width up to 10cm

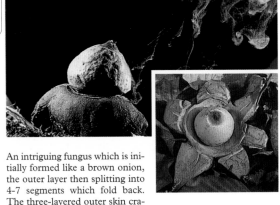

An intriguing fungus which is initially formed like a brown onion, the outer layer then splitting into 4-7 segments which fold back. The three-layered outer skin cracks as it folds back, often leaving an uncracked central disc like a cup in which a central globe, full of spores, sits. There is a pore at the sphere apex through which spores are dispersed when the fungus is knocked or hit by raindrops. Widespread but local in Britain and Europe. It grows in woodlands and hedgerows. It appears from September to November and is not edible.

Common Puffball *Lycoperdon perlatum* Height up to 8cm

The club-shaped fruit body of this distinctive fungus is 2-3cm across at its widest. It is pure white becoming yellowish-brown with age. The surface is covered with short pyramidal spines, each surrounded by a ring of smaller spines or warts giving a netted appearance. The central spore mass is at first white but eventually turns grey-black. With age, a small mouth opens at the apex from which the spores puff out when it is squeezed. Widespread in Britain and Europe. It grows in woods and appears from September to November. It is edible only when the spores are white.

Stump Puffball *Lycoperdon pyriforme* Height up to 5cm

A small puffball which forms large clusters. Each individual puffball is pear-shaped; the size is very variable but averages 2-3cm in diameter and often not much taller. The surface is covered with very small spines which soon fall off, leaving it smooth. The dark spores are discharged through a small central opening when the spores finally mature; heavy rainfall or a sharp blow causes them to puff out. Widespread in Britain and Europe. It is found in woods growing on decaying tree stumps and logs, the only puffball to invariably do so. It is not edible.

Lycoperdon echinatum Height up to 5cm

A distinctive and unusual puffball. The fruit body varies according to stage of maturity from pear-shaped to rounded on a thick stem; the diameter ranges from 2-4cm. The surface of the fruit body is covered in a dense coating of spine-like scales. Young fruit bodies are covered with these scales but, in older specimens, they become detached on the upper surface leaving a pattern like tiny mosaic tiles. Widespread but distinctly local in Britain and Europe. It grows in wooded areas and appears from August to October. It is not edible.

101

Giant Puffball *Langermannia gigantea* Width up to 70cm

An enormous and impressive puffball fungus which can weigh several kilos. It resembles a large, creamy-white smooth football with a leathery outer layer. Eventually, it darkens and splits, and is kicked around by livestock, causing the brown spores to be puffed into the air in clouds. Widespread in Britain and Europe and is locally common in suitable habitats. It grows in grazed meadows and appears from August to October. It is edible and delicious when young and the interior is white; a popular way of cooking this species is to cut it into slices and fry.

Pestle Puffball *Calvatia excipuliformis* Height up to 15cm

This pestle-shaped fungus in easily recognised. Fruit body is a rounded, sometimes almost spherical head, 4-10cm in diameter, which is carried on a tall and stout stem. The surface of the head is covered in flaky, warty scales which are lost with age; the surface ground colour is off-white to cream in the fruit body's early stages but becoming browner with age when the skin at the apex tears allowing the spores to be released. Widespread in Britain and Europe although rather local. It grows in woodlands and appears from September to November. It is edible when young.

Horn of Plenty *Craterellus cornucopiodes* Height up to 10cm

A trumpet-shaped, often tattered-looking fungus. The funnel-shaped cap is up to 8cm across and is irregularly folded and indented, especially around the margin. The horn interior is black when moist but paler when dry. The exterior, which sheds the spores, is grey, the surface textured but lacking gills. The cap grades into the stout, tapering stem and this adds to the fungus's trumpet-like appearance. Widespread in Europe including Britain. It grows in woodland, especially under beech, and appears from September to November. It is edible and good and relatively popular on mainland Europe.

Chanterelle *Cantharellus cibarius* Height up to 10cm

A well-known mushroom, popular with chefs. The cap averages 7cm across and is bright egg-yellow; in its early stages, it is rounded although it tends to become funnel-shaped with age. The under surface appears to have gills but these are in fact branching corrugations in the spore-bearing surface, which is slightly paler than the upper surface. Stem is short, sturdy and paler than the cap. The fungus smells of dried apricots. Widespread in Britain and Europe and locally common. It grows in woodland and appears from September to November. This species is edible and delicious.

Cantharellus infundibuliformis Height up to 8cm

In its early stages, the cap of this species is flattened with a depressed centre; with age, it expands and flattens to an average diameter of 4cm. Although the overall appearance of the mature cap is funnel-shaped, it is often rather distorted or one-sided. The upper surface of the cap is chocolate brown while the underside, on which gill-like wrinkles appear, is pale and bears a network of veins like a cabbage leaf. The stem is yellowish. Widespread in Britain and Europe. It grows in woodland and appears from September to November. It is edible and considered delicious.

Moor Club *Clavaria argillacea* Height up to 5cm

A small and easily overlooked fungus with an appearance like rubber. The fruit body tapers towards the base and is irregularly club-shaped and about 5mm wide with an abrupt ending, often grooved at the apex; it is usually yellowish in colour and often grows in small but tightly packed clumps. The Moor Club is widespread in Britain and Europe but is seldom particularly numerous. It grows mainly on heaths and favours areas with short vegetation and low-growing moss. It appears from October to February and, although edible, is not worth considering.

Fairy Club Fungus *Clavaridelphus junceus* (*Clavaria juncea*)
Height up to 8cm

A filamentous and delicate little fungus which so closely resembles a plant fibre it is extremely easy to overlook unless it is specifically being searched for. The fruit body is incredibly thin and uniform along its length except for the tapering apex; it is pale buffish-brown in colour. Widespread in Britain and Europe. It is a fungus of deciduous woodland and grows on decaying twigs among the leaf litter on the forest floor; numerous fruit bodies grow in a row on suitable twigs. This species appears during September and October and is not edible.

White Coral Fungus *Clavulina cristata* Height up to 7cm

A distinctive and attractive little fungus. The fruit body forms tufts of small clumps of twisted and branched clubs, the tips of which are usually highly divided into smaller branches; the whole effect bears a passing similarity to coral, hence the common English name. The colour is usually pure white although the fungus may darken towards the tips with age. Widespread in Britain and north-western Europe. It grows in both coniferous and deciduous woodland and is found on the forest floor. It appears from September to November and, although edible, is not worth considering.

105

Clavulinopsis luteoalba Height up to 6cm

A striking and attractive little fungus. The fruit body is an orange-yellow, blunt-tipped spindle roughly 3mm thick; the tip may be grooved and slightly flattened and is often paler than the rest of the fruit body. The fungus grows in small clumps and the individual fruit bodies are often curved or distorted depending on the growing postion. Widespread in Britain and north-western and northern Europe; it is often common. The species grows in areas of short grassy or mossy terrain such as lawns and appears from September to November. It is probably not edible so should be avoided.

Giant Club *Clavariadelphus pistillaris* Height up to 30cm

A large strange-looking fungus, the club-shaped appearance of which bears a fanciful resemblance to a pestle. The fruit body is tall and swollen with a slightly wrinkled texture to the most swollen regions; these can be up to 5cm across or sometimes more. The surface of the fruit body is rather smooth and is reddish-brown to dark buff in colour. Widespread in Britain and Europe but everywhere distinctly local. It grows mainly in wooded regions, often under beech on chalky soils, and appears from September to November. It is not edible.

Clavariadelphus fistulosus Height up to 25cm

The fruit body of this woodland fungus is tall and thin, tapering slightly towards the base and expanding slightly towards the tip, the apex of which is usually rather pointed and kinked; it is orange-buff in colour, the colour becoming more intense towards the tip. The base is usually bent or distorted depending on the growing position of the fruit body. Widespread in Britain and Europe but always local and often rare. It grows mainly on the decaying twigs of deciduous trees such as beech and appears from September to February. Although edible, it is not worth considering.

Ramaria stricta Height up to 10cm

This rather striking species is shaped like a miniature bush or a much-branched cactus. The whole fungus is highly divided with multiple branches ascending vertically; these branches are rigid and a pale cinnamon colour, paling further at the tips. This fungus has quite a sweet smell but a sharp and peppery taste. Widespread in northern and western Europe including Britain although it is rather local throughout. It grows on stumps and fallen branches of both deciduous and coniferous trees, often when these are partly buried, and appears from September to November. This species is not edible.

Cauliflower Fungus *Sparassis crispa* Height up to 25cm

The fruit body of this fungus, up to 40cm across, does indeed bear a resemblance to a cauliflower. It comprises a much-branched and curled pale ochraceous-grey globe, perhaps more similar to a large specimen of one of the curly lettuces. The surface is tough and stiff. Widespread in Britain and Europe although usually rather local and seldom numerous. It grows at the base of dead and dying conifers and appears from September to November. It is edible and pleasant, having a taste of aniseed; it is, however, very difficult to remove all the sand that collects between its lobes.

Stereum gausapatum Up to 4cm across

A striking, mat-forming fungus. The fruit body appears superficially rather lichen-like: it is encrusting and forms adpressed brackets that are tough and leathery. The upper surface of the bracket is orange-brown and usually much paler towards the margins; the surface is highly textured. The spore-producing lower surface is much darker and smooth; it 'bleeds' if cut. Widespread in central and northern Europe including Britain. It is usually common and grows on decaying stumps and branches of deciduous trees, particularly oak. This species can be seen throughout the year and is not edible.

Hairy Stereum *Stereum hirsutum* Up to 4cm across

A distinctive fungus comprising tough, flexible brackets that are up to 1mm thick. The colour varies and the species is usually yellow on the underside with the upper surface often zoned in shades of ochre and grey, and covered in fine hairs. Below the bracket itself there may be a variable layer applied flat to the surface of the deciduous wood on which it lives. If the undersurface is bruised by rubbing hard it remains unchanged. Widespread in Britain and Europe. It is a woodland species and can be seen at any time of year. It is not edible.

Stereum rugosum Up to 4cm across

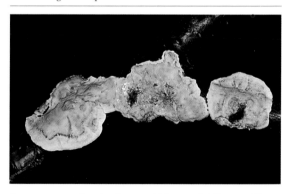

A common, mat-forming fungus which superficially resembles an encrusting lichen. It forms tough and rather woody, inflexible brackets which are up to 2mm thick; these may appear to be attached to their growing substrate across their entire area. The upper surface is pale buff to almost white, sometimes showing concentric zones, rather like the effect of dried water stains on paper. The lower, spore-producing surface is pinkish-buff and bleeds if cut. Widespread in Britain and northern and central Europe. It occurs in deciduous woodland and grows on fallen, decaying branches and stumps. It is not edible.

109

Earth-fan *Thelephora terrestris* Up to 5cm across

An aptly-named fungus which both grows on the ground and produces fan-shaped fruit bodies. The individual fruit bodies are usually 2mm or so thick and they are produced in overlapping whorls and clusters. Reddish-brown base colour darkens with age. The surface is covered in radiating fibres which overhang the edge as a white margin. As it has no means of supporting itself, the fungus climbs up grasses, heather and in fact anything available. Widespread in Britain and northern Europe. It grows associated with the roots of conifers and appears from September to November. This species is not edible.

Wood Hedgehog *Hydnum repandum* Up to 8cm across

Pale buff or cream-coloured cap averages 5cm in diameter. There are no gills on the undersurface of the cap but instead there are many spines which vary from 4-8mm long; these are slightly more pinkish than the cap. The spines are longest halfway in from the edge and run down the stem, becoming shorter there; they are brittle and rub off easily. The flesh has a cheesy consistency and the stem is robust and whitish. Widespread and locally common in Britain and Europe. Grows both in deciduous and coniferous woodland. Edible and considered good by some people.

110

This fungus has spines instead of gills. Large specimens grow in tiered masses, the overall effect resembling the ice seen on a frozen waterfall. The fruit bodies are brackets up to 5cm thick and are usually roughly and irregularly semi-circular in outline. The upper surface is buffish-white with a coarse texture that often collects particles of woodland debris. The under surface is covered with spines which are up to 12mm and slightly paler than the upper surface. Widespread but rather scarce in Britain and Europe. It grows on the trunks of deciduous trees and appears from August to October. Edible, but not worth considering.

Ear-pick Fungus *Auriscalapium vulgare* Height up to 9cm

This fungus resembles a Victorian ear-pick, hence its common name. The cap is usually irregularly semi-circular or kidney-shaped; it is comparatively thick and leathery and is rich brown in colour but darkening with age. The under surface of the cap is covered with coarse spines which are the same colour as the cap at first but become dusted with white spores as they mature. The slightly hairy stem is attached off-centre and tapers towards the cap. Widespread in Britain and northern Europe. It occurs in coniferous woodland, growing on buried pine cones, and appears from September to November. This fungus is not edible.

111

Dryad's Saddle *Polyporus squamosus* Up to 50cm across

An often huge polypore which grows as a large bracket and usually forms large clumps. The individual bracket may be up to 5cm thick at the base. The upper surface is cream-coloured and has large, dark brown scales which sometimes appear to be arranged in concentric circles. The lower surface is covered in creamy-white pores which are large, angular and irregular. The brackets are corky-hard when mature. Widespread in Britain and Europe. It grows on deciduous trees especially sycamore, elm, ash and sometimes beech. It appears from June to September and, although edible, is not worth considering.

Polyporus floccipes Up to 7cm across

This polypore sometimes grows to resemble a bracket fungus but at other times has a cap carried on a distinct stem. The cap is usually irregularly semicircular or even kidney-shaped in outline. The upper surface is pale buffish-brown and is covered in darker, coarse scales. The under surface is covered with cream-coloured pores which are angular and irregular; these run down the stem. The cream stem varies in length and is attached off-centre to the cap. This species is widespread in Britain and Europe but rather scarce. It occurs in deciduous woodland, and appears from April to June. It is not edible.

112

Sulphur Polypore *Laetiporus sulphureus* Up to 40cm across

This species has the intriguing alternative common English name of Chicken of the Woods. The fruit bodies comprise individual brackets which usually have a wavy edge and may be as much as 5cm thick; they are leathery in texture. The upper surface is sulphur-yellow while the under surface, which is covered with pores, is usually more orange. Characteristically, this species grows in large masses of tiered and overlapping brackets. Widespread in Britain and Europe but seldom numerous. It grows on deciduous trees, particularly oak and sweet chestnut, and appears from September to November. Edible and considered good by many.

Burnt Polypore *Bjerkandera adusta* Up to 8cm across

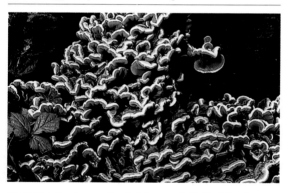

An extremely common bracket fungus. Individual brackets are usually irregularly semi-circular in outline and typically grow in large masses with overlapping and tiered brackets; consequently it can sometimes be difficult to determine which are individual brackets. The upper surface is greyish-brown in colour, the margin usually being pale. The under surface, which is covered with pores, is greyish-white at first but soon looks rather grubby and darker. Widespread in Britain and Europe. It grows on the decaying stumps and branches of deciduous trees and appears from September to November. It is not edible.

113

The fruit body of this rather strange fungus is a large, thick bracket with the texture, feel and appearance of a sponge when fresh. The upper surface is reddish to reddish-brown with paler colouring often in broad, concentric zones; the margin is usually yellowish-buff. The under surface is covered in pores which are yellowish at first but darken with age and run down the tapering stem. Widespread but local in Europe but distinctly rare in Britain. It grows parasitically on conifers and appears from September to November. It is not edible.

Birch Polypore *Piptoporus betulinus* Up to 20cm across

In the past, this bracket fungus was dried and used for sharpening razors, a use which gave rise to its alternative common English name of Razor-strop Fungus. The bracket is semi-circular to broadly rounded in outline and about 5cm thick in the centre. The upper surface is smooth and pale ochre-brown; the under surface is covered with fine pores that are at first creamy-white. The Birch Polypore is widespread in Britain and Europe. As its common English name suggests, it grows exclusively on birch trees and can be seen throughout the year. It is not edible.

114

Many-zoned Polypore *Coriolus versicolor* (*Trametes versicolor*)
Up to 8cm across

Perhaps the common-est bracket fungus in the region. Each bracket is broadly semi-circular, often with a lobed margin; it is usually only 2mm or so thick and has the upper surface zoned in many colours, the overall hue ranging from buffish-pink to black; the texture is silky in the bracket's early stages but this disappears with age. The underside is pale buff and is covered with fine pores. Common in Britain and Europe. It grows on all types of fallen and decaying deciduous wood and can be found at any time of year. This species is not edible.

Pseudotrametes (*Trametes*) *gibbosa* Up to 15cm across

This thick bracket fungus has a corky texture. Each bracket is roughly semi-circular in outline, up to 15cm deep and 8cm thick. The upper surface is whitish, the margin sometimes appearing creamy. The lower surface is covered with pores which are radially elongated and creamy. The species can be recognised by the fact that algae rapidly colonise the upper surface, turning it green. The bracket is rapidly attacked by insect larvae. Occurs throughout Britain and Europe. It grows on decaying deciduous wood, especially beech, and appears in September and October. It is not edible.

115

Blushing Bracket *Daedelopsis confragosa* Up to 20cm across

A common and distinctive bracket fungus. Each bracket is usually semi-circular in outline, up to 10cm deep but thickening to only 2cm. The upper surface is concentrically zoned, initially buff to cinnamon brown, then darkening and at length becoming rusty-red. The pores on the underside are at first creamy-buff and bruise pink when fresh, but later become grey. Occurs in Britain and most of northern and central Europe. It grows on most deciduous trees but is most common on sallow and willows and appears from September to November. Inedible.

Root Fomes *Heterobasidion annosum* Up to 25cm across

A parasitic polypore that is potentially life-threatening to the host tree. The brackets are large and usually highly irregular in outline and overall shape, being up to 12cm wide and up to 2cm thick. The upper surface often looks swollen and lumpy and is reddish-brown in colour; the margin is usually whitish as is the under surface which is covered with pores. Widespread in Britain and parts of northern and central Europe. It grows on the roots of conifers, at first on living trees, later killing these. It can be found at any time of year and is not edible.

116

Rigidoporus ulmarius Up to 50cm across

A common bracket fungus. An individual bracket is large and irregular in shape although roughly semi-circular in outline; it is tough and woody, up to 12cm deep and up to 8cm thick at the centre. The upper surface is extremely bumpy and uneven, the depressions and cracks harbouring woodland debris and sometimes acquiring a coating of algae. The under surface is covered with pale buff pores, the margin sometimes appearing more intense in colour. Common and widespread in Britain and Europe. It is found growing low down on deciduous trees, and can be found throughout the year. It is not edible.

Ishnoderma resinosum Up to 25cm across

The bracket of this unusual fungus is roughly semi-circular in outline, up to 12cm deep and up to 3cm thick. The upper surface is undulating and the margin is slightly wavy and folded down when viewed in profile; it also yields red resin when young and this collects in droplets around the margin. The underside is covered with creamy-white, angular pores which darken with age. Occurs in Britain, where it is rather scarce, and in Europe. It grows on the dead stumps of coniferous and deciduous trees and appears from September to December. It is not edible.

117

Phellinus ignarius Up to 35cm across

A parasitic bracket fungus. The bracket is roughly semi-circular or even kidney-shaped in outline when seen from above but thick and hoof-shaped when seen in profile; it is up to 8cm deep and 20cm thick. The upper surface is reddish in young specimens but becomes a dark greyish-brown with concentric folds with age; the margin may appear paler in young specimens. The lower surface is covered with orange-buff pores. Occurs in Britain and Europe but is generally local and uncommon. It grows on deciduous trees, especially willows, at any time of year. It is not edible.

Inonotus radiatus Up to 8cm across

A medium-sized bracket fungus which sometimes forms fairly extensive tiers. Individual brackets are up to 5cm deep and up to 2cm thick. They are woody and tough with an upper surface that is fairly smooth and orange-buff in young specimens but darkening considerably with age. The lower surface is covered with whitish-buff pores which spread downwards among the tiered brackets. Widespread in Britain and Europe but rather local. It grows parasitically, mainly on alder, appearing on the trunks and persisting throughout the year. This species is not edible.

118

Ganoderma adspersum Up to 50cm across

A common, tier-forming bracket fungus. Each bracket is roughly semi-circular in outline with the margin slightly lobed; it is up to 20cm deep and up to 15cm thick. The upper surface is reddish-brown with concentric folds and ridges. The under surface is covered with pinkish-white pores which shed brown spores that stain the brackets below and the tree trunk on which they are growing. Widespread in Britain and Europe. It grows parasitically on the lower trunks of deciduous trees and can be found throughout the year. It is not edible.

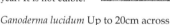

Ganoderma lucidum Up to 20cm across

The bracket of this fungus is roughly kidney-shaped with a lobed and wavy margin. Upper surface is smooth but uneven with concentric zones of reddish to dark brown or black; it is shiny and looks varnished. The under surface is covered with circular off-white pores which gradually darken with time. The bracket is sometimes borne on a stout and rough stem. Widespread in Britain and Europe but local and scarce in most regions. It grows on the roots of deciduous trees, appearing to grow on the ground if the root is buried. Found throughout the year and is not edible.

Artist's Fungus *Ganoderma applanatum* Up to 45cm across

A large bracket fungus which earns its common English name because the lower surface can be drawn on. The bracket is roughly semi-circular in outline, up to 30cm deep and 5cm thick. The upper surface is uneven and knobbly, being made up of concentric growth layers; it is reddish-brown, often with a pale margin. The lower surface is pale-buff and bruises easily. Widespread in Britain and Europe but generally rather local and scarce. It grows on deciduous trunks such as beech and can be seen throughout the year. This species is not edible.

Hoof Fungus *Fomes fomentarius* Up to 35cm across

An aptly named hoof-shaped fungus. The upper surface is grey, ridged and zoned with paler brown towards the lower margin. The pores are light grey-brown and the flesh, and indeed the whole fungus, is extremely tough and rigid. Because of its hard texture, this perennial fungus was used as tinder in the past. Most common in the Highlands of Scotland, where it grows on birches; in southern England and mainland Europe, it is much scarcer and usually found on beech. It can be seen at any time and, not surprisingly given its tough nature, is not edible.

120

Beefsteak Fungus *Fistulina hepatica* Up to 12cm across

The texture and colour of this rather rubbery bracket fungus have a passing resemblance to a blood-dripping beefsteak. The bracket is a deep reddish colour when young, rather like uncooked liver, but later it becomes more rigid and darkens. In the young state, it oozes drops of blood-like fluid. Widespread in Britain and Europe but rather local. It grows on oak trees; the mycelium does not destroy the tree but colours the wood to make the desirable 'brown oak' of cabinet makers. It appears from June to September and, despite its appearance, is edible and considered good by some.

Phlebia merismioides (P.radiata) Up to 10cm across

A distinctive, mat-forming and superficially lichen-like adpressed fungus. The fruit body forms extensive roundish to oval, but always irregular, patches which overlap, fuse and become generally difficult to discern as individuals. The surface is rubbery and ridged, bright orange-red in colour usually with a distinctly paler margin. Widespread and common in Britain and most of northern and central Europe. It grows on the bark of dead deciduous trees, especially birch and beech, and appears from November to February. This species is not edible.

Ear Fungus *Auricularia (Hirneola) auricula-judae* Up to 8cm across

An unusual and distinctive, gelatinous fungus. It is partly translucent when viewed against the light and is often distinctly ear-shaped. The hollow of the 'ear' faces downwards and the back often shows branched wrinkles which resemble veins. It is tan in colour and felty in texture on the upper surface; the lower surface is smooth and grey-brown. Widespread in Britain and Europe and sometimes rather common. It grows on deciduous trees and is commonest on elder trunks and branches, fruiting right through the winter. Although edible, its unappetising appearance puts most people off.

Tremella foliacea Up to 8cm across

A strange fungus with a jelly-like texture which can resemble a miniature brain in fully formed specimens. The fruit body consists of an irregular gelatinous mass which is slimy and convoluted; it is reddish-brown to purplish-brown in colour when fresh but darkens as it dries, becoming blackish-brown. Common and widespread in Britain but less so on mainland north-western Europe. It is a woodland species which is found growing on the dead branches of deciduous trees such as oak. It appears from November to March and is, not surprisingly, inedible.

Yellow Brain Fungus *Tremella mesenterica* Up to 10cm long

A conspicuous and distinctive jelly-like fungus. The fruit body consists of a convoluted, brain-like mass that can be up to 4cm wide; it is bright, clear yellow and the species is very eye-catching in a winter setting. As the fruit body ages, it dries and darkens to orange-brown, losing its jelly-like texture. Widespread in Britain and Europe. It is especially common on gorse in heathland settings but is also often found on many kinds of deciduous wood, usually on branches that are dead but have not fallen. It appears from November to March and is not edible.

Witches' Butter *Exidia glandulosa* Up to 5cm across

A strange fungus with fruit bodies that are shiny and gelatinous, and which fancifully resemble blackened knobs of butter hence its common name. It is similar in overall shape to Yellow Brain Fungus but is all-black and forms brain-like lumps. Its shape differentiates it from the black, jelly-like *Bulgaria inquinans* as does the fact that a finger wiped across its surface does not become black with shed spores. Common and widespread in Britain and north-western Europe. It grows on deciduous wood, especially on oak, and can be seen at any time of year. It is not edible.

Yellow Stag's-horn Fungus *Calocera viscosa*
Height up to 8cm

A well-named fungus which is branched and bears a passing resemblance to an antler. Size varies greatly from small growths only 2cm high to larger, tree-like structures. The colour is bright egg-yellow causing the fungus to stand out conspicuously on the woodland floor; with age, it dries and darkens. This species is common and widespread in Britain and northern and central Europe. It occurs almost exclusively in coniferous woodland, growing firmly attached to decaying stumps or partly buried roots. It appears from September to November and is not edible.

Morchella costata Height up to 12cm

A distinctive, medium-sized fungus, one of several rather similar species of morels. The cap is rounded-conical and tall, up to 9cm in height, while the apex usually rather rounded and indented. The surface of the cap is deep brown in colour and covered in depressions which are defined by ridges that lie between the conspicuous, almost parallel, vertical ribs. The stem is whitish and textured, the flesh being hollow. Widespread in central and southern Europe. It grows on open ground, sometimes on rather disturbed soil, and appears in the spring. This species is edible and considered delicious.

Morel *Morchella esculenta* Height up to 30cm

This distinctive fungus is one of the most highly regarded and prized edible species in the region. It is extremely variable in size and the rounded to pear-shaped head is pale fawn and wrinkled, the surface honeycombed with deep depressions; the cap texture is spongy. The stem is white and thick, often swollen towards the base. Widespread in Britain and Europe but rather uncommon. It is found in a variety of habitats from sand dunes to chalk woodlands, but appears to prefer alkaline soils. It appears from March to May and is edible and delicious.

Common Morel *Morchella vulgaris* Height up to 14cm

A distinctive species which is extremely variable both in terms of its size and its shape. The head is irregularly rounded or pear-shaped, the apex sometimes having a pointed tip; the colour is pale buffish-brown. The surface is wrinkled and convoluted with a honeycombed network of deep depressions and ridges; the overall effect somewhat resembles a bath sponge. The whitish stem is robust and usually irregularly distorted. Widespread in Britain and Europe but, despite its common English name, is rather uncommon. It grows in wayside areas and appears from March to June. It is edible and delicious.

125

Mitrophora semilibra Height up to 8cm

A very variable fungus; some specimens could even be passed over as small Stinkhorns. The cap is irregularly conical in shape or sometimes rather rounded. It is covered with conspicuous, almost parallel, vertical ribs between which there are sunken cross-ribs; the cap colour is brown, the ribs normally appearing darker. The white stem is variable in length but usually rather swollen towards the base. Widespread in Britain and Europe but rather local. It grows in damp woodland and appears from March to June. Although edible, it is not worth considering.

Common Helvella *Helvella crispa* Height up to 15cm

A rather strange-looking and distinctive fungus whose cap makes it easy to recognise. The cap itself may reach 12cm or more in large specimens but is more usually about 8cm high. It is very pale grey to creamy-white; it is curly and may vary greatly in shape, but always sits on a deeply furrowed white stem whose distorted shape and texture recalls extruded plastic. Widespread in Britain and Europe. It grows in deciduous woodlands along grassy rides or in leaf litter and appears from September to November. Although edible, it is not worth considering.

False Morel *Gyromitra esculenta* Height up to 12cm

Another extraordinary-looking fungus which superficially resembles a morel. The cap or head is reddish-brown and is usually irregularly rounded but can be almost any shape. The surface of the head is covered with convoluted folds and lobes, much more rounded in outline and more densely packed than true morels; the overall effect can resemble a small brain. The stem is white, robust and usually distorted. Widespread in Britain and Europe but is rather uncommon. It grows on sandy soils and appears from March to June. This species is poisonous when raw and should therefore be avoided.

Peziza vesiculosa Up to 8cm across

A distinctive, cup-shaped fungus, one of several similar-looking species. The cup has a textured and smoothly wrinkled surface, the inrolled margin adding to the vessel-like appearance; the margin is usually tattered and torn. Some specimens retain their almost spherical shape although many become distorted. The outer surface is pale buffish-brown with a powdery texture while the inner surface is slightly darker, showing small blisters with age. Widespread in Britain and north-western Europe. It grows on substrates such as compost heaps and rotting leaf litter, appearing from September to April. It is not edible.

Peziza cerea Up to 5cm across

A fleshy, cup-like fungus perhaps most easily distinguished from other similar species by its preferred growing habitats. The cup is usually distorted and pale creamy-buff in colour. Both surfaces are more-or-less the same colour but the inner surface is smooth while the outer surface has a dusty texture. The fungus often grows in clusters or groups in suitable habitats. Widespread in Britain and Europe and sometimes quite common. It grows most conspicuously on the mortar between bricks and paving stones and can be found at almost any time of year. It is not edible.

Peziza petersii Up to 5cm across

An irregularly cup-shaped fungus which is often found growing in sizeable clusters in suitable habitats. The cup is often compressed with the opening rather restricted and frayed; in some specimens or clusters, there is a resemblance to clams or other shellfish. The cup colour is buffish-tan; the outer surface is usually greyish towards the base. Widespread but rather uncommon in Britain and Europe. It grows in a wide range of wayside settings but often on ground that has been burnt. This species appears from June to October and is not edible.

Peziza badia Up to 7cm across

A fleshy and fairly distinctive cup fungus. Compared to many of its relatives, the cup is open and rather shallow, the margin usually being wavy and sometimes torn. The inner surface is dark reddish-brown while the outer surface is slightly paler with a dusty texture. Widespread and sometimes common in Britain and Europe. It grows on the ground where the soil is heavy and often compressed by trampling and appears from August to October. It is poisonous when raw but apparently edible when cooked; this species is probably best avoided.

Scarlet Elf-cup *Sarcoscypha coccinea* Up to 5cm across

This colourful and distinctive fungus grows as well-formed cups or bowls. The inner surface of the cup is bright scarlet with a smooth texture; by contrast, the outer surface is very pale with a chalky or downy texture. The cup is attached to its growing substrate by short but tough fibres. Widespread in Britain and northern and central Europe, although it is seldom numerous. Found beside woodland paths on the forest floor, apparently growing from the ground; closer examination will reveal an attachment to fallen or partly buried wood. It appears from January to May and is not edible.

Hare's-ear *Otidea onotica* Height up to 10cm

A distinctive and attractive fungus with a fancifully descriptive common English name. The lop-sided, elongated cup does indeed resemble the ear of a hare or rabbit. The surface is often rather crinkled and the margin eventually becomes frayed. The inner surface is orange-flesh coloured and smooth while the outer surface is yellow with a powdery texture. The whole fungus is attached to the ground by a short stem. Widespread but rather local in Britain and Europe. It is found in deciduous woodland and grows among the leaf litter. It appears from September to November and is not edible.

Otidea alutacea Up to 4cm across

This fungus forms lop-sided cups which are usually less distorted than the superficially similar Hare's-ear fungus. The cup is sometimes almost bowl-shaped but is usually irregularly shaped with a wavy margin. The inner surface is buffish-orange to pale tan in colour while the outer surface is paler and rather mealy. The cup is attached to the ground by a very short, thick stem. Widespread in Britain and north-western Europe but rather scarce. It grows in woodlands, sometimes forming clusters among the leaf litter. It appears from August to October and is not edible.

130

Orange Peel Fungus *Aleuria aurantia* Up to 8cm across

This highly distinctive fungus is the brightest of the more common cup-fungi. It forms rather irregularly shaped cups of various sizes from 1cm upwards. The inner surface is bright orange and the outer surface is orange-grey; the overall effect is similar to orange peel turned inside out. When collected it may give off a puff of spores like smoke as all the asci discharge simultaneously. Widespread in Britain and northern Europe. It grows on the ground amongst grass or leaves in a range of habitats and appears from September to November. It is not edible.

Mitrula paludosa Height up to 4cm

A strange and intriguing little damp habitat fungus. The spore-producing head is rounded or club-shaped and bright yellow or yellow-orange. It is carried on a long, slender white stem which may be distorted depending on the growing position; in many situations where this species grows, it is only the yellow head that is clearly visible. *Mitrula paludosa* is widespread in Britain and northern Europe but generally rather local and easily overlooked. It can be found in a variety of damp habitats and characteristically grows through *Sphagnum* moss. It appears from April to July and is not edible.

131

Green Wood Fungus *Chlorosplenium (Chlorociboria)*
aeruginascens Height (fruit body) Up to 2mm

Well known for the green-staining effect it has on its growing substrate and for the tiny green fruit bodies it produces. The fruit bodies of the fungus are bright verdigris green; they are flattened or
cup-shaped and about 1-5mm across. The mycelium of this fungus stains the wood green and is more often seen than the fruit
bodies. The coloured wood was formerly used in the decorated
boxes known as 'Tunbridge Ware'. Widespread in Britain and
Europe. Grows on fallen timber of deciduous trees, especially oak,
and can be found throughout the year. It is not edible.

Bachelor's Buttons *Bulgaria inquinans* Up to 4cm across

Each black 'jelly-blob' of this fungus consists of a thick circular
body, averaging 1cm in diameter, which becomes a rounded top-
shape; this is brownish at first on the sides and black on the upper
surface. The fungus can be differentiated from the superficially
similar *Exidia glandulosa* by its black spores, which come off on the
finger; the latter has clear spores. Widespread in Britain and
Europe and often common. It grows in rows along the bark of
recently fallen oak and irregularly on the bark on beech. It appears
from September to November and is not edible.

Ascocoryne sarcoides Up to 1cm across

A common, jelly-like fungus. It consists of reddish-purple 'jelly-like blobs' which are clustered together and recognisable by their colour. Not all of them become mature or reach the 'perfect' stage but when they do they become top-shaped, about 1.5-2cm across, with a flat upper surface. Widespread in Britain and northern Europe and is locally numerous, sometimes forming extensive clusters. It is a fungus of deciduous woodlands and grows on the bark, and sometimes the wood, of fallen beech and other trees. This fungus appears from September to November and is not edible.

Bisporella citrina Up to 2mm across

A distinctive and often common fungus, sometimes forming dense and extensive patches. Each fruit body is round and disc-shaped on its upper surface, tapering to a narrow base; fresh specimens are bright yellow while older specimens darken or fade. On suitable substrates, this species forms clusters with the individual fruit bodies often touching and appearing to merge. Widespread in Britain and north-western Europe. It is a woodland species and is found growing on the fallen branches and timber of deciduous trees, often where the bark has peeled away. It appears from September to October and is not edible.

133

A rather variable, jelly-like fungus. The fruit body can be anything from 2cm upwards and comprises a fleshy mass with a convoluted and irregular surface; the colour is usually pinkish-brown and the surface is rather smooth, the outermost face being rather smooth. The fungus sometimes forms dense clusters. Widespread in Britain and Europe and sometimes locally common. It is a woodland fungus, being found growing on dead branches and twigs of beech and other deciduous trees. It appears from August to November and is not edible.

Perigord Truffle *Tuber melanosporum* Up to 5cm across

This is possibly the most flavoursome and highly prized of all fungus species. The fruit body is an almost spherical but often lumpy mass; the surface is blackish and shiny and is covered in angular, warty patches. When cut, the flesh appears dark bluish-brown but marbled with white veins. The Perigord Truffle does not occur in Britain but is widespread in southern Europe. It is subterranean, occurring in oak woods, and so consequently is seldom seen unless specifically searched for. Pigs and trained dogs are used by commercial truffle hunters. It is edible and delicious.

134

Dead Man's Fingers *Xylaria polymorpha* Height up to 8cm

A strange-looking fungus whose appearance often befits its rather unappealing common English name. The fruit body consists of irregular and rather distorted club-shaped spikes which bear a passing resemblance to a human finger. The surface is blackish and rough in texture. The 'finger' is carried on a stem-like spike which is buffish-brown. This fungus is widespread in Britain and Europe. It occurs in deciduous woodland, especially under beech, and grows on rotting stumps. It appears at any time of year and is not edible.

Candle-snuff Fungus *Xylaria hypoxylon* Height up to 6cm

One of the most common and easily identified of all fungi to be found on dead wood. It consists of flattened, black stems which arise vertically from the wood; these usually, but not always, branch into two- to five-pointed antler-like extensions. At first these are white and then, as they mature, they blacken so eventually the whole fungus is black. On suitable substrates, clusters of fruit bodies occur. Widespread in Britain and Europe. It is a woodland species which grows on the decaying stumps and branches of deciduous trees. It can be found throughout the year and is not edible.

135

A tiny, cluster-forming fungus. The fruit body is a small domed or hemispherical structure which is rusty-red at first but then becomes black with age; the surface is minutely rough. As the red phase is short lived and tends to occur in late summer, the fungus is usually encountered later in the season in the black state, in which it is very persistent. Widespread in Britain and Europe and often common. It grows on the bark of dead beech, occasionally on other deciduous trees, and appears from September until at least November. It is not edible.

Coral Spot Fungus *Nectria cinnabarina* Up to 3mm across

A tiny but extremely colourful fungus which is invariably seen in clusters, these sometimes covering large areas of the growing substrate. The fungus occurs as two stages which are sometimes seen growing side by side. The asexual stage consists of attractive pinkish-orange cushions while the sexual stage is cinnabar-red and hard. Widespread in Britain and Europe and often very common. It grows on all types of fallen and dead twigs, branches and stumps, and can be seen at any time throughout the year. This unusual fungus is not edible.

Cordyceps ophioglossioides Height up to 10cm

An intriguing and easily overlooked parasitic fungus. The fruit body is irregularly club-shaped. The surface is minutely warty in texture and yellow in its early stages; it becomes blackish with age although the stem on which it is borne often remains yellowish. The stem is often twisted or distorted depending on the growing position of the fungus. Widespread in Britain and northern Europe but local and generally uncommon. It grows on the subterranean, truffle-like fungus *Elaphomyces muricatus* and is found in woodland. It appears from September to November. Inedible.

Cordyceps canadensis Height up to 10cm

This is a rather unusual and distinctive parasitic fungus. The fertile part of the fruit body comprises a shiny, reddish-brown swelling which is rather conker-like and is borne on a long stem. The stem itself is bright yellowish-orange and is often rather twisted or distorted depending on the growing position of the fungus. Local and rather uncommon in Britain and northern Europe. It is parasitic on subterranean, truffle-like *Elaphomyces* fungi and grows in coniferous woodlands. It appears from September to November. This is not an edible species.

This distinctive and knobbly fungus is also known as Cramp Balls because of its old reputation for curing cramp. The fruit body forms in successive layers and appears as round, shiny black lumps. At first, these are covered with a reddish spore layer but this washes off, leaving the black surface. If the fungus is cut in half it will be seen to be composed of concentric layers of very dark to very light grey material. Widespread in Britain and Europe. It grows on ash or rarely on other deciduous trees and can be found throughout the year. It is not edible.

Ustulina deusta Up to 4cm across

A common encrusting fungus which has a passing resemblance to a mat-forming lichen. The fruit body consists of a patch which is roughly rounded but extremely irregular in outline and with a wavy and indented margin. In its early stages, the fungus is greyish-brown with the margin usually paler; it is rather brittle. Later it darkens to almost black and becomes extremely brittle. Widespread in Britain and Europe. It grows on the decaying stumps of beech and other deciduous trees, and appears in its grey form from June to August; the blackened form persists longer. It is not edible.

Wolf's Milk Fungus *Lycogala epidendrum* Up to 1cm across

A strange-looking fungus which is the fruiting stage of a Myxomycete fungus, or slime mould. For most of its life, the fungus occurs as a mass of protoplasm but in this readily identifiable stage is seen as globular masses, usually clustered together; these are pinkish in their early stages but fade and eventually split to reveal and liberate the spores inside. Widespread in Britain and Europe. It is a woodland species which grows on dead wood, especially of deciduous trees. This fungus is most often seen from July to September and is not edible.

Fuligo septa Up to 7cm across

One of the most brightly coloured of all slime mould fungi. Its colour is the best feature for distinguishing this from other species. For most of its life, the slime mould comprises undistinguished and amorphous protoplasm. Like others of its kind, the protoplasm of this species comes together to form a soft, jelly-like mass; it is bright yellow and the consistency of this mass is so soft that it can barely stay together. Widespread in Britain and Europe. It is a woodland species which is found oozing over or smothering wood between March and June. It is not edible.

Further reading

The books listed below are inexpensive, well-illustrated guides on the subject.

Bon, M., *Mushrooms and Toadstools of Britain and Northwestern Europe*. Hodder and Stoughton, London, 1987.

Dickson, G. *Green Guide to the Mushrooms and Toadstools of Britain and Europe*. New Holland, London 1992.

Lange, J. and Hora, F.B., *Collins Guide to Mushrooms and Toadstools*. Collins, London, 1963.

Pegler, D., *Mushrooms and Toadstools*. Mitchell Beazley, London, 1987.

Philips, R,P., *Mushrooms and Other Fungi of Great Britain and Europe*. Pan Books, London, 1981,

Sterry, P.R., *Fungi of Britain and Northern Europe*. W.H.Smith, London, 1991.

Useful addresses

There is only one society in Britain concerned with the study of fungi, both amateur and professional:

The British Mycological Society
General Secretary: Dr A.J.S. Whalley
School of Natural Sciences
Liverpool Polytechnic
Byrom Street
Liverpool L3 3AF

The society publishes a magazine, *The Mycologist*, which aims to promote an interest in fungi in people of all ages and interest levels.

Most County Naturalist's Trusts hold field meetings, often referred to as 'Fungus Forays', in the autumn and there is usually an expert in attendance to help identify difficult specimens. Addresses of these Trusts can be obtained from local libraries. The body that represents them collectively is:

The Wildlife Trusts
The Green
Witham Park
Waterside South
Lincoln LN5 7JR

Index